THE FOLLOWER EFFECT

A Story About Flipping the Script on Leadership

By Tony A. Bridwell Ed.D
Author of Saturday Morning Tea and
The Do Over

Copyright © 2024 by Tony Bridwell
Copy Edit: Stephanie Kemp
Editorial Work: Mindi Bach
Interior Design: Sleigh Creative
Photo Credit: Shelbie Whitten
Cover Design: Sean Langel

All rights reserved. No part of this book may be reproduced in any form or by any electronic or mechanical means, including information storage and retrieval systems, without written permission from the publisher, except for a reviewer who may quote brief passages in a review.

Paperback ISBN: 979-8-9863747-2-7
Hardback ISBN: 979-8-9863747-4-1
Ebook ISBN: 979-8-9863747-3-4

Printed in the United States of America. All rights reserved under international copyright law. Contents and/or cover may not be reproduced in whole or in part in any form without the express written consent of the publisher.

THE FOLLOWER EFFECT

A Story About Flipping the
Script on Leadership

By Tony A. Bridwell Ed.D
Author of Saturday Morning Tea and
The Do Over

To all who are called to lead, may you also excel in the humility and wisdom it takes to follow.

PROLOGUE

THE UNFORESEEN CLASSROOM

"Sometimes the most profound transformations are hidden in the places we least expect."

BLAKE

Blake reclined in the overstuffed leather chair, staring intently out his office window. He swirled an exquisitely carved glass of 12-year-old bourbon—the spinning ice rock hypnotically timed with his racing thoughts. In spite of the softening glow outside the window, his mind was wrestling with both contempt for his adversary and the words of wisdom from a colleague. Usually, crushing his competition was the only chess move worthy of contemplation. Yet Erin's last words drew him into an uncharacteristic moment of reflection as he faced the final negotiations for his biggest deal in industry history.

She was the lead director on his board; her words were never hollow. A former high-potential talent that Blake had mentored through the first season of her career, Erin was one of the few who understood the ins and outs of Blake's business and how he works. There was no fast-talking with industry jargon to impress the other members when Erin was in the room. She knew his moves and had played the high stakes game of business chess with Blake for years. Erin's resilient spirit had always been a worthy opponent for Blake—a man some would label the tumultuous brilliant jerk.

For Blake, power has been his weapon of choice. As CEO of a fast-growing tech company, local media has held him up as the darling of the city, enabling his power plays and control struggles. No one paused to seek the *true* story, the one behind the scenes, and understand how Blake could manipulate Wall Street investors into a shark-infested frenzy.

Blake's success was built on the antithesis of all his father taught him. For Blake, the idea that power and control were THE most effective ways to navigate dealing with people formed his core values. This was an ethos that Blake leaned into, most would say, to prove his father wrong. His father, known to generations of students as *the Professor*, modeled a way of life that manifested true power through influence—a strategy largely lost on Blake's narcissistic tendencies.

The Professor personified a power that did not originate from a place of positional authority, but rather from the more influential position of followership. Blake, however, could never shake the story in his head that followership was a sign of weakness and passivity. It was this belief that set the course for Blake's journey and a lifetime of trying to prove his father wrong.

His father had always taught that an entrepreneur has three unique traits that manifest at different levels of intensity. First, they have an exceptional skill or talent that sets them apart from the pack. Second, they have a vision for the future that few can see. Finally, they can work with people in a manner that brings out the very best in what they have to offer. The average entrepreneur has one of the three; the good ones have two of three. But it is the rare, exceptional entrepreneur that has three for three. Of the three, the elusive skill of dealing with people tends to be what stands between good and great.

Blake was a solid two out of three, and he was just fine with that. His idea of dealing with people more resembled the sadistic drill sergeant that had only one goal—push others to achieve his goals at all costs and with all the force required. After all, he reasoned, there are a dozen people who will kill to have a seat around this table. This was Blake's mantra. He said it so many times the team had coffee mugs made at Christmas printed with those words.

Now, as dozens of lawyers and analysts were working countless hours in the final weeks leading up to closing his largest deal—the merger that would announce to the world Blake's total dominance in the marketplace—Blake faced another crisis of belief. All that he knew, or thought he knew, was being challenged by Erin. His mind raced to process the feedback and focus on the one constant he was sure of: the data. Yet a strange, unfamiliar sensation was consuming his mind. He had made room for emotion—compassion even—and it was troubling him.

As he took another sip of his drink, his gaze settled on the picture on his desk. Maybe it was the bourbon or just an overwhelming confluence of emotions, but he couldn't take his eyes off the photo in the old wooden frame. In a blink, the picture transported Blake's thoughts to another moment in time—one where life converged like two streams and became a single current. Blake recognized the timely message in the photo and its immediate impact on life. With an eye on the horizon, he knew he had to make a decision that could change everything.

BLAKE AND LEAH

Blake eased the century-old door ajar, slipping into the back of the auditorium-style classroom. He paused behind the last row, hoping to go unnoticed. Years had passed since his last academic encounter and a rush of adrenaline surged through him as familiar sights, sounds, and the musty scent of the room ignited long-forgotten college memories. Yet a new, distinct sensation set this day apart—a mix of surprise and curiosity about what lay ahead. Unbeknownst to him, crossing the threshold of that classroom would chart a course toward a future beyond his wildest dreams—a transformative journey that would alter his life's trajectory.

Blake took a seat in the upper section. His eyes descended past the gentle cascade of rows and rested at the heart of the auditorium. To the side of the projector stood a familiar and commanding figure—a tall, lean presence with shoulder-length silver hair, each strand catching the light. Her attire and poise were impeccable—the kind that commanded attention and graced fashion covers.

Blake's vision sharpened as the figure spoke, confirming what he already knew. It was indeed Leah, the architect of Blake's early career and the mentor who had steered him through corporate storms. Leah's transition from the boardroom to the classroom hadn't lessened her impact. Instead, it transformed her legacy to also include a tribute to a revered professor and mentor whose wisdom remained vivid in the minds of those who had known him. Leah's experience blossomed into a living memory in this space; her teachings were a silent symphony to Blake's father who had mentored her.

Blake refocused his attention on the over-sized screen in the front of the room. In sleek white letters on an ink-black backdrop were the words "*The Follower Effect.*" He looked down at his email and was reminded of a conversation with Erin weeks earlier at the end of a bone-jarring board meeting.

While standing in the empty cavernous room on the 31st floor of the mid-town office tower, Erin's patience with Blake's toxic behavior was running thin. Her insights for Blake were direct and to the point. She had enough votes on the board to remove him as CEO and she would use them if he didn't change his toxic ways.

"You have to learn to be a follower if you are going to effectively lead at the next level." Erin's words were still ringing in Blake's head.

Unaccustomed to the receiving end of an ultimatum, Blake was rocked back on his heels from the sheer jolt of hearing the words. Erin stopped him before he could even consider moving his lips to respond.

"Blake, I am dead serious. You have one shot. If you don't apply the same energy to this as you do to pushing your people to the brink of exhaustion, then you are out!" she said with a force that seemed to surprise even her.

Startled, yet silently impressed with the chutzpa from his former protégé, he mustered a reply.

"What exactly do you want me to do?"

For a split second, it was there—barely perceivable—but for Erin, she picked up on the hint of vulnerability in Blake's response. Was it possible, that somewhere inside the brilliant jerk was a heavy heart seeking refuge from the bondage of his ego? She recognized a man, shackled to his belief that he had to demonstrate his worth by proving to his father that he was right. Years after his father's death, Blake was still consumed by the toxic story in his head.

In a surprise move, Erin called in some favors and arranged for Blake to enroll in Leah's class at the university—far away from his company and his routine. For nine weeks, Blake would attend class, interact with his fellow classmates, and complete the assignments just as any student would be required to do. A good report from Leah would be the evidence the board needed to allow Blake to remain at the helm of the company.

As Leah lectured at the front of the hall, it became apparent that the Follower Effect would be a challenging story to learn. Blake watched Leah pull the class into her every word as his mind filled with memories of days gone by. Before he was old enough to attend university, Blake slipped into his father's classes to watch the man he idolized early in life. It's difficult to find an exact time when everything shifted.

Reaching into the company-branded backpack Erin gave Blake before he left, he retrieved a journal. As he opened the front cover, he noticed the words written in Erin's script: "To all who are called to lead, may you also excel in the humility and wisdom it takes to follow."

> "To all who are called to lead, may you also excel in the humility and wisdom it takes to follow."

Below the inscription, she had continued:

"Blake, I found this quote in a book your father wrote. I honestly believe that if you learn to follow well, you will find a sense of hope and joy you have yet to discover. I am your biggest cheerleader and advocate. The future is bright, and the best is yet to come. Erin."

WEEK ONE

THE FOUNDATIONS OF FOLLOWERSHIP

"The Follower Effect is the inseparable duality of leadership and followership roles within individuals.

Blake entered the charming tea shop—not his normal respite after navigating boardrooms and high-rise offices. He had been on a fast-moving learning curve ever since stepping into the life of an entrepreneur at an early age. While school was—well, just that—Blake always felt that true learning happened in the hustle of the marketplace. While not wrong, he had forgotten that there was also a tremendous amount of learning that happens in other settings.

The pungent smell of freshly roasted coffee triumphed over the aromas of Earl Gray and Bengal Spice teas. After housing multiple enterprises for six generations of customers, the old structure was converted into a little shop catering to the varied desires of loyal clientele. Individuals from diverse backgrounds had discovered the diminutive shop to satisfy their early morning cravings for pastries and coffee.

Leah's presence was announced by a jingle of the old brass bell hanging atop the storied door. She confidently made her way to the antique table where Blake had been waiting. Blake stood as Leah approached and they gave one another a long, compassionate embrace—the kind that bridges the time that has kept friends apart. Leah settled in her chair and met her friend's eyes.

"Blake, it warms my heart to see you in class," Leah began as a disheveled student working her way through school arrived to take their orders.

"Good morning, Professor!" The server's familiarity with Leah was evident. "The usual?"

"Yes, Mindy," Leah replied with a warm, inviting smile. "And for my friend, who is new to our little oasis, he will try the Bengal Spice tea this morning. And bring him one of your famous blueberry scones." Leah gave Blake a wink.

"I have to admit, it has been a while since I had a hot tea and a blueberry scone," Blake said uncomfortably.

"I shared many a-cup-of-tea and scones with your father over the years." Leah's smile was compassionate.

Mindy placed two porcelain cups and saucers and the light pastry on the table.

"Thank you for meeting with me," Blake said, picking up his teacup without using the handle. "Full disclosure—it sounds like your approval of my progress will be important when this class is over, so I'm hedging my bets with this one-on-one."

"My pleasure, Blake." Leah laughed. "The ground rules are simple. You attend class, collaborate with your cohort, put in the work, and once a week, we will meet to debrief your progress." Leah forked her first bite of scone.

Blake nodded, contemplating the rules of engagement.

"So, where do you want to begin?" Leah asked.

Blake took his first bite of blueberry scone, and the tension in his shoulders and neck began to subside. In a rare moment of vulnerability, he leaned in.

"I also used to share tea and scones with Dad. Honestly, it's been a while and this moment is a bit surreal."

Leah smiled. "I know. It seems we are both having the same experience."

They both chewed in silence.

"So, what have you learned after the first week?" she continued, glancing over the top of her tea.

"I hear what you are saying in class about followership. Dad had a similar point of view." Blakes voice was halting, and Leah could sense his lack of conviction.

Leah set down her scone.

"Blake, we need to grasp the true meaning of following before we can fully embrace the new concepts surrounding it. True followership involves the seamless transition between leading and following, representing a singular role with dual aspects—not isolated positions."

> "True followership involves the seamless transition between leading and following, representing a singular role with dual aspects—not isolated positions."

Blake's face told the full story—he wasn't fully convinced.

"So, it's not just about following directives, but also about contributing to the leadership process?" Blake asked, still pondering the dualistic role of followership.

"Exactly," Leah replied. "Imagine it as a dance in which you easily alternate between leading and following. It's about participating actively in both capacities and allowing the process to mold you, as well."

Like all dances, this was one in which Blake had never learned the moves.

"That means, as a follower, I'm not just receiving guidance but also influencing and adding value to the process?" Blake pondered. The idea made sense intellectually, but was still foreign to Blake.

"Yes, and this is the point at which an individual's contributions and insights are useful," Leah offered. "A good follower actively participates in the leadership process by contributing their own thoughts and viewpoints, in addition to carrying out tasks."

Blake nodded and slowly sipped his tea, considering Leah's words.

"So, based on class this week, real followership involves learning from one another and developing together—with the role of the follower becoming just as important and dynamic as a leader."

Blake reached for his notebook and dug through the notes until he found the page that confirmed his last statement.

"Indeed!" Leah grinned, impressed by Blake's thorough notetaking given his position. "And the ideas we put into practice will be built around this understanding. It's about giving each team member the freedom to accept their dual roles as both followers and leaders."

"So, we need to ensure a solid foundation to fully understand The Follower Effect." Blake's tone was confident, but still unconvinced.

"People are the center of every culture," Leah continued, eyeing Blake as he casually jotted down a note. "The ability of the people to learn, unlearn, and relearn is the leading indicator of a healthy culture."

Leah glanced over her tea to catch a glimpse of Blake with an ever-so-slight nod of approval.

"So, development is essential?" Blake paused from taking notes.

"Yes, a person's learning capacity is necessary for thriving individuals and a healthy culture," Leah responded. "Three learning principles form the foundation of followership." Leah was holding up three fingers with her right hand and then paused to take a sip of tea so Blake could catch up on his notes. "These learning principles are fundamental to the

Follower Effect and are necessary for the effective follower."

PRINCIPLE NUMBER ONE

"Principle number one." Leah, now holding up a single finger on her right hand, prompted Blake to break down sub-headings. "Never assume everyone knows what you know at the level you know. This is where your journey to reshape the organization begins."

> *Principle Number One*
> *Never assume everyone knows what you know at the level you know.*

Blake nodded with a bit more understanding as he wrote.

"We inevitably limit communication in multiple directions when we make these assumptions," Leah continued. "Instead of encouraging clarity and inquiry, it fosters a culture of silence and presumption. Sharing knowledge is important, but so is making sure it is understandable and available to everyone."

Blake considered this idea in light of his personal experiences. He tended to be a directive leader who did not value collaborative discussion. Without taking into account the team's varying degrees of knowledge, he would issue commands and compile lists and expectations while unfairly anticipating prompt understanding and compliance.

"I can see how It could lead to a disconnect," murmured Blake, continuing to write as he processed. "We bypass the opportunity to interact, impart knowledge, and benefit from one another. Consequently, our team members are traveling at varying speeds and frequently in separate directions."

"That's right," Leah nodded. "Inadequate comprehension of an idea by an individual can result in mistakes, blunders, and, eventually, a collapse in the group's output. However, it doesn't have to be this way. You can empower your team when you take the time to make sure everyone understands. This establishes a common language and a common course of action."

Blake set his pen down and considered this principle's wider ramifications.

"So, this pertains also to me and all of us who hold positions of authority?"

"Precisely. It's critical to remember our dual role, which allows us to move fluidly between leading and following," Leah confirmed. "As effective followers, we have an obligation to engage with the information we are given and shape it into something understandable and useful for both ourselves and those we impact. Then, as a result, a two-way learning dynamic is created, enabling each member to contribute their knowledge and questions. It's about opening up the culture to a mindset of mutual growth, where everyone contributes to and gains from common knowledge, and the lines between leader and follower become less distinct. That's the core of the Follower Effect: setting an example and purposefully following."

As Leah's spoon tinkled softly against the porcelain, her eyes glistened with a mixture of wisdom and mischievous challenge.

"Blake, cultivating understanding is the first step towards transforming any organization and, in fact, any area of influence within the organization. It's similar to this tea." Leah raised the kettle and poured more liquid into their cups. "To guarantee the ideal blend, each component needs time to simmer and release its essence."

Blake watched the tea's amber color deepen, a visual representation of Leah's allegory. He began to realize that his job required him to do more than simply impart knowledge into people's heads—like teabags into boiling water—and hope for fast absorption. He could grasp the need to be more deliberate and patient, like Leah, but previous success made for a cruel teacher.

Leah leaned closer.

"Blake, these moments are similar to tea rituals. They infuse the practice of followership with vitality and rhythm. Let's draw this out together so you can grasp this concept."

Blake continued journaling and brainstorming ideas for how to incorporate these techniques into their boardroom and team dynamics.

"It's more than just clarity, isn't it?" he pondered out loud. "It's about deep, meaningful connections with each other, all while focused on the organization's shared goals."

Leah nodded.

"Yes. It's about making sure that everyone travels the same route of understanding—uniting behind a common goal." Leah's voice became more passionate. "The core of the Follower Effect is when a team, even in a boardroom, becomes a true community rather than just a space for people to exchange empty words back and forth between each other. Every person is a part of a missional orbit, pulled together by a common gravitational force towards an objective that is far bigger than any one agenda."

Leah paused thoughtfully.

"But watch out for the *brilliant jerk* trap: those who, even when acting as followers, maintain a selfish independent orbit and interfere with productive teamwork by pursuing their own goals."

Blake looked up sharply, knowing to whom Leah was referring. She smiled and took another sip of tea. The blended flavors of the tea created a nuanced balance that illustrated the harmony of a group of people working toward a common goal. Blake took a last sip and relished the warmth and well-balanced complexity reflective of their discussion.

Both of them finished their treats and rose to depart. Blake was silent, still contemplating the challenges to his thinking after his debrief. It was subtle, but it did feel like the fog was about to clear. He'd figured he'd better pace himself, though, as it was only the first week.

"We have only scratched the surface of the First Principle of Followership today." Leah smiled while guiding Blake towards the door. "I look forward to our follow-up conversation next week."

They stepped outside in lock step with the sound of rusty cowbells hanging from the handle, startling Blake.

"Maybe in the future, I can pick the spot." Blake winked at Leah and reached over to silence the bells.

"I'll consider it." Leah smiled and put on her jacket. "Remember, Blake, this is just the first layer of the learning. There are still unanswered questions and more concepts to incorporate into the conversation regarding leadership and followership. We will unravel the remaining strands together once you put these lessons into practice and observe them in action."

As Leah departed, Blake waved with his journal, which now held a veritable gold mine of notes. He stepped out into the crisp air, leaving the ancient tea shop behind him and sensing a journey full of promise ahead. Blake knew he had to figure out how to integrate this first principle into the core of his work. It was time to think things through, reconsider his current mindset, and then take action.

BLAKE'S JOURNAL NOTES TO ERIN

Erin:

I can't believe I'm saying this, but thank you for this assignment. Contemplating my first class with Leah, I couldn't help but think about how effective followers are always in learning mode. This resonates deeply with me, sparking a moment of clarity. The framework Leah gave us in class has become a framework to guide my learning journey. Here is the **Reflect, Rethink, Act model**.

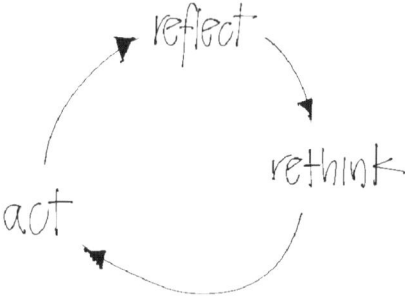

The model is simple yet powerful, and I think it will serve as a good check point for us each week.

The model begins with **Reflect**. *This is where I pause to think deeply about my actions. Two questions to ask to begin my reflection: What was my energy and what was my emotion? When I consider my energy, I think about what gave me energy and what depleted my energy. When I consider my emotion, I think about what surprised me, and what frustrated me. Reflection is about gaining insights from experiences and understanding small wins and smart failures.*

Next, I **Rethink***. This phase is about learning from reflection and using that knowledge to evolve. It's about personal and professional development, adapting strategies, and improving skills. Growth ensures that how I* **Act** *is more informed and effective.*

The next step IS to **Act***, where I will take concrete actions based on current knowledge and situations. This is about stepping into the unknown, trying new strategies, and being proactive in my role.*

This model isn't just a tool for me; I've been told it's a potential coaching guide for anyone on any team. It encourages continuous learning and adaptation, essential qualities in a dynamic leadership environment.

The more I consider it, the **Reflect, Rethink, Act model** *can also serve as a compass for our organization as we all navigate the complex waters of leadership and teamwork. Like these weeks for me, it's a testament to the power of learning - a journey that begins with doing, enriched by reflection, and culminates in growth. I thought sharing the* **Reflect, Rethink, Act** *with you each week could open up new possibilities for us, as well.*

Stay tuned…

BLAKE'S JOURNAL NOTES TO HIMSELF

"Now What" Moment: Cultivating Comprehension

1. *Dialogue Circles: Begin by establishing 'Dialogue Circles' within our teams—a safe space where each member can voice their understanding of the mission and the 'why' behind it. Like the circles formed by pebbles in a pond, these discussions can ripple out, expanding collaborative understanding throughout the organization.*

2. *Teach-Backs: Implement 'Teach-Backs' where team members explain concepts or strategies in their own words. It's like tasting the tea to ensure the flavor is just right. This practice not only confirms comprehension but also reveals new insights.*

3. *Understanding Checkpoints: Set up Understanding Checkpoints. These are regular intervals where you pause and reflect, ensuring everyone's cup is filled to the same level with knowledge and purpose. It helps prevent misunderstandings from seeping into the fabric of the team.*

WEEK TWO

THE LESSON IN LEARNING

"The Follower Effect highlights how each person simultaneously embodies both influencing and being influenced to co-create organizational culture."

Blake took his time as he strolled down the tree-lined promenade. The lively energy of academic life provided a refreshing contrast to the corporate offices he normally inhabited. The crisp fall day ignited his thoughts as he meandered through the 100-year-old Georgian architecture. He pondered how his recent encounters would impact his leadership abilities as the shift in thinking seemed substantial. He also thought about what he had built.

Who could argue with those results?

He eventually arrived at the Dallas business school where students were milling around, eager to catch Leah's attention. Leah moved among them, tall in stature and equally as confident. The word on campus about Leah's class had spread and the classroom was not only full of students but also a visiting professor or two.

At just over six-feet tall, Blake towered over most of the students. He waved, catching Leah's attention—a casual move to let the professor know her special student was in class that day.

"Blake, it's so good to see you." Leah pushed her way through the students. She held a bag and cup high over her head. "Today's class has a full agenda. Why don't we plan to connect right after to discuss."

"Only if you let me pick the location." Blake smiled. "We agreed on that yesterday."

Leah gave him a thumbs up as she pushed back into the magnetic crowd.

Much like last week, Blake feverishly took notes through the hour-long lecture. Afterward, once the buzz of class and student meetings had waned, Blake made his way down from the upper reaches of the room.

"Your popularity continues to grow," Blake smiled. "I might need an upgrade to premium seats soon."

Leah blushed and shook him off, deflecting the compliment.

"I do believe I am the one following you today," she said.

Blake held open the door.

"You up for a short walk?" He noticed Leah's raised eyebrow, curious about their potential destination.

Heading down the main boulevard of campus, the two crossed University Street and headed over towards the city. Blake guided them to the section, just off campus, where establishments have been serving the community for well over a century. After a few blocks, Blake slowed to a stop in front of the Burger House.

"I haven't been here in years!" Leah looked pleased.

Blake pulled open the door and they made their way into the tiny space that had been recognized by the city as the best hamburger in town. Ordering and grabbing a rare open table, the two retreated with their baskets brimming with burgers and fries. Blake produced extra napkins for the table as Leah chuckled out loud.

"Are you trying to tell me something?" she said as she picked up an extra napkin for her lap. "I'm a pretty careful eater."

"If memory serves, like any good burger joint, we may both need a few extra to handle these." Blake grabbed another one for himself.

Blake cradled the massive burger with two hands, hovering over the basket as he prepared for the first bite.

"I've spent time this week strategizing how to put Principle One into practice with my team," Blake said while using one of the napkins to capture a juicy drip on his chin. "And honestly, it's been difficult."

Leah took a big bite and chewed on his words. It was apparent by her body language that she was loving this change of menu.

Blake held his burger in one hand while carefully selecting the right fry to dip into the ketchup. Leah paused, holding her burger carefully over the red basket in order to make intentional eye contact with Blake.

"Thank you for being so transparent." Her voice was reassuring. "As you well know, we find some of our greatest success navigating through difficulties. Don't give up."

As both continued with their next bite, it gave them time to fully consider the moment.

"I've known you long enough to know that you have most likely worked out some tool or model to help you navigate the challenge," Leah said.

Blake nodded with a slight grin, still chewing.

"That's the one thing Dad taught me that sort of stuck."

"I suspect there is more than one thing that's stuck if you really think about it." Leah smiled while attempting to conceal morsels from her final bite.

Producing his journal from his backpack, Blake pulled on the black ribbon that marked an important page. He handed it to Leah, and she was able to see Blake's notes and drawing of the *Reflect, Rethink, Act Model* along with his notes for Erin.

Studying the model closely, Leah's eyes brightened with approval.

"Blake, this is amazing. An ideal instrument for lifelong learning."

Blake visibly relaxed as he let the recognition of his work wash over him. He was used to compliments, but many of them were hollow at times as people tried to manage his unpredictable moods. This moment was different coming from Leah.

PRINCIPLE NUMBER TWO

"Blake, this is a perfect segue to the main idea of class today. Principle Number Two: Never assume you know all there is to know."

Principle Number Two
Never assume you know all there is to know.

Retrieving his journal back from Leah, Blake thumbed a few pages to find his notes from class.

"My takeaway from this principle is understanding that knowledge is ever-evolving, and we must always be open to learning," Blake read from his notes.

"Excellent!" Leah exclaimed. "It's important to also acknowledge that this principle goes beyond knowledge for its own sake. It hinges on accepting the humility that results from realizing that knowledge is constantly changing. We must continue to learn about our profession, the business, and human nature in our role as both followers and leaders."

Blake immediately thought of the arguments he had with Erin—the tension caused by inflexible opinions and the deadlocks that ensued. He started to recognize that their conflicts frequently resulted from a mutual unwillingness to admit the boundaries of their knowledge.

"This can be a hard pill to swallow," Blake mused as he picked at the last remaining fry in the basket.

"Erin and I have had our fair share of disagreements—most of them over topics like this."

"Welcome to the human race," Leah said with a smile. "That admission, in itself, is a sign of maturity. Leading with conviction and following with the curiosity of a lifelong learner is a carefully synchronized dance in leadership. We create a culture where progress is welcomed and expected when we let go of the need to be the all-knowing leader and commit to lifelong learning."

For the next half hour, they explored related topics about the value of keeping an open mind, continuing to be inquisitive, and realizing that every encounter presents an opportunity to learn something new about the industry, other people, and ourselves. Leah summed it up with just two words before picking up her cup to take the last drink of her sweet iced tea.

"Intellectual humility."

Blake tapped his pen on his notebook and then jotted down a note to himself.

Watching Blake, Leah set her drink down and leaned forward, pointing to a new page in the notebook.

"To navigate the ebb and flows of our professional journey effectively," she said, "we need to build a learning community with three types of support: collaborators, coaches, and counselors."

Blake paused and looked up.

"That sounds like the *Three C's* of community if I can use some alliteration. Can you elaborate on that for me?"

"That's a great memorization tool," Leah said with a smile. "Collaborators walk with us, providing a sounding board and sharing the practical experiences that come with tackling daily tasks. Coaches join us for a season, aligned with specific goals to elevate our performance. These partnerships can be significant, and brief."

Leah paused so that Blake could catch up.

"And counselors," Leah's voice grew softer. "They provide us with the insight to understand the bigger picture and the secure haven to sort out the complexities of life. Whether they are knowledgeable mentors or accomplished professionals, they are the confidants who help us make sense of our path."

> "We need to build a learning community with three types of support: collaborators, coaches, and counselors."

Blake made the final notes on the page. Then, placing his pen in the middle of his journal, he looked at Leah.

"Thank you for that clarification. I've never fully appreciated the multiple roles you have played in my life from the time I was young." Blake was uncharacteristically personal. "After Mom passed away, I never really let anyone get close to me. But you were always there as an early collaborator when I wanted to launch out on my own, as a coach once the business began to grow faster than I could manage, and to some degree, as a counselor—especially during my career."

He paused for a moment.

"Thank you," he continued softly, twisting the edge of his napkin.

Leah grabbed her own napkin and gently dabbed the corners of her eye.

"Good thing you got those extra napkins." She smiled as she controlled the dam threatening her eyelids.

"Blake, the ability to stand confidently in what you know, while being acutely aware of what you don't, is the genuine test of a leader and follower. It's about taking the lead in a humble manner and jumping at the chance to learn more. That is what you are experiencing. Don't miss that." Leah neatly folded her napkin and placed it on the table.

Blake finished his notes and realized that accepting his own intellectual shortcomings might help him communicate more effectively, providing a route to more cooperation and creativity. It was becoming obvious that to proceed, he would have to walk out his day fully aware of intellectual humility. Blake was discovering a stronger connection to the Follower Effect and how this impacted his work with his team, the board, and the prospect of the future merger.

"Help me unpack one of your comments from class today," Blake said as he picked up his pen. "I'm curious about your phrase: *autonomous critical thinking*."

"Absolutely. Great observation." Leah smiled again. "Being an autonomous critical thinker has three key attributes."

Blake turned to a new page in his journal as Leah finished off her drink.

"The critical thinker is **constantly curious** about life while being **keenly self-aware** of their own beliefs and biases, **willing to rethink** and reevaluate their thoughts and feelings based on new information as appropriate," Leah said. "The independent critical thinker will voice a constructive concern in an effort to support the mission."

Blake started to combine the strands of autonomous critical thinking with the tapestry of intellectual humility as he thought about what Leah had said. It would require constantly testing one's comprehension and evaluating and synthesizing new material while never assuming total knowledge. It served as the cornerstone for the development of autonomous critical thought.

Blake looked up from his journal.

"Is it safe to conclude that becoming a critical thinker is indispensable to this learning mindset—carefully analyzing what we already know, challenging the existing status quo, and not running from uncertainty?"

"Absolutely," Leah said. "It calls on us to distinguish between opinion and reality, evaluate the reliability of our sources, and interact with different points of view—even when they contradict our own. Your insight is crucial, and learning to interact with the data critically is about examining, analyzing, and proving it."

"Well, that is interesting," Blake said before setting down his pen down.

Leah could sense that her old friend was still processing the information.

"I have always considered myself a critical thinker, but truth be told, I am not sure I've always been willing to rethink my own position. I've been more concerned about how I defend my position." Blake confessed.

Leah paused, recognizing the beginning of a self-awareness journey that held great potential for the future.

"Let's capture some of these insights," Leah said, capitalizing on the momentum.

As Blake concluded the list, Leah was encouraged. Her true desire and hope for Blake was that these were more than mere words in his journal, and that they would become the new habit of his life. Leah knew that, in life, habit always wins."

"In life, habit always wins."

"Thank you so much for the burger." Leah smiled at Blake as they exited the eclectic bistro.

"You are very welcome, my friend. I guess that means that next week, it's your pick." Blake squeezed her shoulder as they strolled back to campus.

Later that night, Blake composed and sent an email to Erin. It had been awhile since he had been in an environment that caused him to think at this level. He began to slowly realize how much he enjoyed solving problems and devising ways to navigate challenges. Maybe it had been the pressures of life that got in the way, but whatever the reason, reluctantly, he recognized that his old habits may be undermining his ability to extract the best from his people.

BLAKE'S JOURNAL NOTES TO ERIN

Erin, here are my notes from the week:

1. *Encourage Continuous Learning Sessions: Make continuous learning a staple within the team dynamics. Integrate it into our regular meetings. The learning model is an excellent tool for this. Remember, continuous improvement is built upon the foundation of continuous learning.*
2. *Build the 3 C's of Community: Be intentional to include collaborators, coaches, and counselors in my community of people.*
3. *Followership is anchored in autonomous critical thinking: I need to be constantly curious, keenly self-aware of my own biases and willing to rethink—and possibly reframe—for the constructive betterment of the mission.*

Reflect: *I've learned that collaboration is about working together and co-evolving in our knowledge and skills. Coaches are not permanent fixtures but rather seasonal guides for specific growth phases. On the other hand, counselors—whether they are mentors or professional therapists—help navigate through complexities.*

Rethink: *Today's dialogue with Leah made me rethink how I view our learning ecosystem. I recognized the need to actively engage with collaborators, coaches, and counselors to enrich this environment. I also see the value of the learning model as I formulate my thoughts. What might be missing is a frame-*

work to allow me to coach others in a way that leaves them better than I found them (not necessarily a methodology I am used to).

Act: *While my current methods are more directive, Leah has encouraged me to consider what it looks like to be an autonomous critical thinker. This requires me to be constantly curious, keenly self-aware of my biases, and willing to rethink and potentially reframe my mindset for the constructive good of the mission. Admittedly, this is not my strong suit and certainly not a habit. So, if I had a model or framework that could guide my thinking, it could lead to more meaningful conversations— maybe a* Curious Coaching Model.

BLAKE'S JOURNAL NOTES TO HIMSELF

Curious Coaching Model Reflections

To provide a simple coaching/conversational framework that supports independent critical thinking, I have outlined a concept called the curious coaching model.

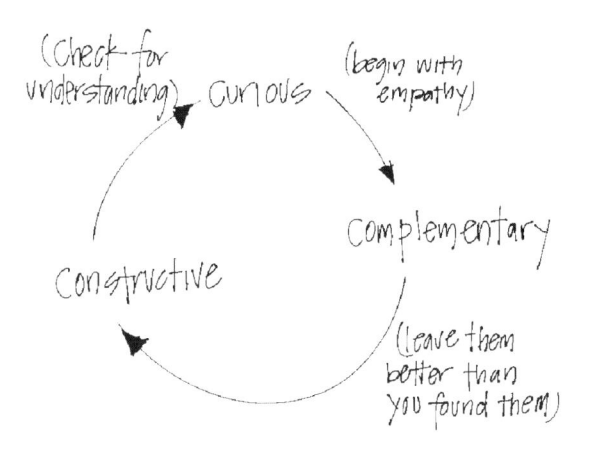

Curious (Check for understanding) → *Complementary* (begin with empathy) → (Leave them better than you found them) → *Constructive* → (back to Curious)

Start with Empathy: *This is where every coaching conversation should begin. First and foremost, I've realized that in order to guide someone properly, I need to understand them—not just what they say but also the feelings and experiences that underlie it. It's about getting to know them on a deeper level and genuinely experiencing the world through their eyes.*

Curiosity: *Next, I need to move into a curious state. Rather than providing instant fixes, I pose open-ended, exploratory questions meant to promote introspection. This is about their journey, NOT mine. The questions serve as a mirror, reflecting to them their ideas and guiding them along the way.*

Complementary: *After we've discussed their experiences and heard their views, I provide a complementary perspective. This is a validation that others are heard and making progress. (Admittedly, this is not one of my stronger attributes)*

Constructive: *The concept of being constructive should include critical thinking that moves the mission closer to its goal. It's an offer of suggestions to rethink or reframe for improvement that builds on the strengths we've both acknowledged. It's not a critique. It's a path forward that they can decide to take, armed with the knowledge and self-assurance we've established together.*

One thought has guided me as I have considered this framework:

The currency of the coaching conversation is clarity. This framework should lead to greater insight and clarity that unlocks either personal, professional, or organizational potential.

The core of a coaching conversation philosophy is to leave them in a better state than when you found them. It's about improving their general well-being as much as their professional acumen. This approach will serve as a lighthouse for the rest of us, directing our team to grow and succeed rather than just work.

Every meeting and every exchange are steps in this process of progress. Putting these ideas down on paper is leading me to wonder what we can accomplish as a team.

WEEK THREE

THE PRINCIPLE IN PRACTICE

"True followership involves the seamless transition between leading and following, representing a singular role with dual aspects—not isolated positions."

Blake entered the boardroom early. The sun was rising, casting a golden hue over the city, promising a quiet and peaceful day for those outside. He needed to be at class the next day but had business to handle before heading out.

"This is it, Erin," Blake said. "This deal might redefine our entire industry. We have to move quickly."

Erin examined Blake's mannerisms. It had been a few weeks since he had started Leah's class, and Erin was curious to see what, if any, navigational shifts Blake may have acquired.

"Blake, I can see you're very enthusiastic about this. I still say it's a risky move."

"Exactly!" Blake nodded. "It's audacious and creative. We must stay on the cutting edge." His intensity seemed uncontrolled.

"I'm curious, what possible risks, in your opinion, are involved?" Erin asked carefully. "Have we thought through every scenario?"

Blake hesitated. His first thought was to immediately push back. But something inside him prompted a momentary pause for reflection. Nodding thoughtfully, Blake realized that Erin was using the curious coaching model.

He let her press on.

"Your ability to recognize these types of opportunities has gotten us this far, Blake, but would a more thorough examination be worthwhile? Maybe a closer investigation will highlight some insights we haven't yet thought about."

Erin paused to gauge how Blake was responding to her coaching.

"I'm curious as to what you think," she said, carefully executing the curious coaching conversation.

Blake's defenses were shattered.

"Well done, Erin." He offered a slight grin of approval.

"I have to admit, your model is simple and effective." Erin stood and walked around the board table to meet Blake.

The usual tension in the space was remarkably absent as Erin made her way to the wall of windows where Blake stood. Blake, who was normally uncompromising, appeared to be considering Erin's words with a new level of intensity.

"Alright, let's investigate more closely. I feel like you are stretching my analytical muscles today," he said. "However, Erin, I'm telling you, we can't let this chance pass us by."

Blake stepped toward Erin, extending his hand as both an expression of learning and challenge.

"I agree on all counts," Erin said carefully. "And thank you for leaning into your learning. It is noticed and much appreciated."

For the first time in years, Blake experienced a sensation of satisfaction in a conversation that he didn't control.

THE LUNCH ENCOUNTER

Later that week, Blake met Leah for lunch after class. He reflected on the coaching conversation Erin had with him, framing the conversation from his perspective. Leah listened quietly, absorbing the nuances of the story.

"First, I want to commend you on your notes from last week and the coaching conversation model. Well done," Leah said. "Coaching a brilliant mind like yours isn't easy. Your willingness to pause to reflect and rethink was actually a testament to *your* growth into effective followership."

Blake pulled out his journal while the table was cleared, encouraged by Leah's words.

"Frequently, the most effective classroom is not on the university campus but in the spaces where we live life. What do you see as your takeaways from your experience with Erin?" Leah asked. "These are important milestones on your journey."

Blake began to make a few notes as they waited for their server to bring them their coffee. With Blake-like precision he shared his takeaways with Leah.

"These are great, Blake." Leah set down her spoon and folded her hands on the table. "Now, talk to me about what you heard in class today."

PRINCIPLE NUMBER THREE

Blake thumbed through his dog-eared journal to find the most recent page.

"At the beginning of class, I jotted down Principle One: Never assume everyone knows what you know at the level you know. And Principle Two: Never assume you know all there is to know."

"Excellent recall." Leah said.

Blake tapped the page where he had scrawled his thoughts on today's lesson, his finger resting on the header

"Principle Three," he cleared his throat, preparing to articulate the concept that had only just begun to crystallize in his mind. "Never confuse knowing with understanding. It's a distinction I hadn't fully grasped before."

Principle Number Three
Never confuse knowing with understanding.

Blake paused and a trace of frustration colored his next words. "Now, I see the root of so many missed expectations. I've been gauging others' knowing of information, presuming it equates to understanding. That was a false, base assumption."

"Excellent insights." Leah thoughtfully probed further. "What do you feel is lacking from your epiphany?"

Blake paused, less certain, his fingers idly flipping back through the previous pages.

"To me, the *why* behind it all isn't clear." His brow was furrowed in thought.

"Unpack that," Leah encouraged, encouraging him to delve deeper.

Blake met her gaze, searching for the right words.

"True understanding," he began, "stems from connecting what we know with why it matters. The significance behind the facts."

Leah nodded, acknowledging his progress in thinking.

"Indeed, understanding is the linchpin of sound decision-making," she added. "It transcends mere accumulation of facts, demanding that we interpret and assimilate the knowledge in order to grasp how it resonates with individuals and influences operations."

She leaned forward for emphasis.

"When you move from knowing to understanding, you open doors to empathy, innovation, and ultimately, transformation. That's the core of both genuine leadership and the Follower Effect."

Blake listened carefully, and silently finished taking notes. What he recorded had become much more than words on a page.

> *"When you move from knowing to understanding, you open doors to empathy, innovation, and ultimately, transformation."*

Leah and Blake packed up and stepped into the cool air. While strolling together, Blake pondered how "understanding" was the path they would all travel together and "knowing" was only the beginning.

"An effective follower," she said, "operates within a mission and purpose orbit, contrasting sharply with the self-centered orbit that can consume leaders and followers alike."

Blake thought about how his career had developed and how the dynamics of the company had brought him to this position. Once a shining example of visionary leadership, Blake began to realize how he had progressively moved into a self-orbit, one where his choices increasingly favored his own goals over the goals of the group. This inward approach hindered his effectiveness, which also started to seep into the company culture and led to a subtle but noticeable disengagement.

> *"An effective follower operates within a mission and purpose orbit, contrasting sharply with the self-centered orbit that can consume leaders and followers alike."*

"An orbit around mission and purpose implies that our decisions and actions are rooted in the organization's larger objectives," Leah said thoughtfully. "It implies that our job is to advance the objectives of the entire business rather than furthering our own personal agendas."

Blake quietly absorbed the additional insights.

"It would seem that a mission-driven strategy helps to transcend small-time politics and self-interest. On the surface, it would appear to create a unifying force that propels group efforts toward a common goal," Blake commented.

"This is one of the reasons I continue to teach." Leah's smile widened. "It is truly remarkable when I can experience my students making the information a reality in their own lives.

She stopped for a moment and put her hand on his shoulder.

"Remember, the essence of the Follower Effect in action is stepping outside one's ego to accept a role that benefits something bigger than oneself. This role requires selflessness, purposefulness, and an unwavering dedication to the organization's ideals and goals." Leah dropped her hand and the two continued to walk along the sidewalk towards their cars.

> *"The essence of the Follower Effect in action is stepping outside one's ego to accept a role that benefits something bigger than oneself."*

Blake slowly realized that he had drifted, ever so gradually, off-center from his purpose. By not paying attention to the culture, he allowed it to slip into a notably unhealthy state. He would need to lead the efforts in building a culture in which the purpose, mission, vision, and values served as the central axis around which all activities revolved. This would then build confidence that every choice, project, and innovation would be a step toward achieving the organization's overall goal.

Blake's mind was full of the day's discoveries. More than just a theory, the Follower Effect provided him with a useful framework for navigating his interactions with Erin and the board. He felt more confident to take on the obstacles ahead since he knew *and* understood the importance of empathy, learning, and communication.

Blake began to grasp the fact that his modeling of leadership was lacking. To navigate back to the transformational leader he desired, he needed to set an example based on the rules of successful followership. Although the road ahead seemed difficult, Blake had the means to make this year of transition into one that would benefit all parties by providing a legacy of development and achievement.

BLAKE'S JOURNAL NOTES TO ERIN

1. *Embrace the Balance of Coaching:* Effective coaching involves a balance between challenging and supporting, especially when dealing with strong personalities.
2. *Growth Through Tension:* The tension in difficult conversations can catalyze growth for both the coach and the individual being coached.
3. *Patience and Persistence:* Change in perspective requires patience and persistence, especially in a brilliant jerk. It's a gradual process of nurturing insight and understanding.

Reflect: *Reflecting on this week, I realize the importance of not confusing knowing with understanding. It's become clear to me that while knowledge is crucial, it's only the surface layer of true comprehension. Understanding delves deeper, seeking the information's significance and the "why" behind the information. This discovery has shed light on my frustration with unmet expectations, prompting me to recognize that I've been measuring others' knowledge when I should be fostering their understanding.*

Rethink: *I must re-evaluate how I communicate expectations and share knowledge with the team. Instead of simply relaying information, I should facilitate discussions that explore its meaning and relevance. It's about creating a dialogue where the team can engage with the material, ask questions,* *and make connections to their work and the larger objectives of our organization.*

Act: *Going forward, I will implement a new approach to leadership and collaboration.*

WEEK FOUR

THE EMOTIONAL AWARENESS IMPACT

"High EQ cultivates self-awareness, intellectual humility, and the capacity to be a strong follower, serving as a defense against bad leadership."

Erin's stiletto Louboutin's echoed across the marbled interior of Blake's only business rival. She traversed the shimmering Dallas building with mixed feelings of excitement and trepidation. The lobby was opulent with high-gloss white floors reflecting the delicate light of brass chandeliers and modern artwork attractive to the building's creative residents.

Her meeting with the executives of TechNova was a delicate balance of assessing the possibility of an acquisition, while also helping to guide Blake as he confronted a disrupter in the industry. TechNova was keen on maximizing Blake's company value with new technological innovations. Blake was already in the boardroom, where the quiet energy of agreements being struck and futures being shaped permeated the air. Erin saw that Blake's opportunity to shine amid the city's ambitious skyline made the meeting essential.

Blake was engrossed in a lengthy conversation with CEO Jonathan Reed and his group. Erin joined them and quickly engaged in talking points and methods that batted around like a protracted rally at the US Open.

As the meeting dragged on, Erin sensed something wasn't quite right. Rather than coming to an agreement, the conversation appeared to be veering off into arguments and subliminal acts of arrogance. Though each leader was intelligent in their own right, they were all unwittingly adding to the mounting emotional chaos.

For Blake, the previous weeks had forced a new way of thinking into his negotiation style, leaving him struggling to find his footing. While he was intent on leveraging his new insights, the muscle memory of years of self-centered behavior came to the forefront.

Erin carefully observed Blake's interactions, laced with brilliant jerk residue that had been his baseline for years. While she was still hopeful, admittedly, the day reminded her of a professional PTSD moment.

Somehow realizing that old habits were dominating the conversation, Blake asked if they could adjourn the meeting until next week. This move took everyone by surprise—including Erin—as Blake would normally wear his prey down, not allowing any time to breathe or regroup. Taking full advantage of the moment, Jonathan seized the opportunity for a brief withdrawal.

Once the group cleared the conference room, Blake reached for his phone to text Leah.

"Any chance you can grab dinner this week before class?"

Leah, having known Blake long enough, recognized that this was a rare, vulnerable moment.

"The Mansion, at 8:30," Leah replied immediately.

Blake placed his phone on the expansive boardroom table and reclined in the leather chair, flooded with relief.

"You okay?" Erin asked tentatively, not wanting to disturb his own ability to self-correct.

"I actually think I am," Blake replied, his eyes focused on the view outside. "Could probably just use a moment to reflect, if you don't mind."

Erin smiled to herself and gathered her things.

"Not at all," she said, quietly slipping out of the room.

THE DINNER

Later that night, Blake and Leah tucked themselves into the Mansion restaurant's antique splendor. Encircled by the gentle radiance of dimmed lighting, they found themselves enveloped in a setting that fused Dallas' colorful history with its dynamic present. Rich, dark wood adorned the walls, while bright patterns glowed in stained-glass windows, perfectly capturing the city's eclectic spirit. Amidst the dishes of handcrafted food and the faint murmur of Dallas' power elites sipping their bourbon neat, Blake narrated the experience of the day.

"It felt like I was watching a ship slowly sink," Blake recounted, as shadows formed on the barreled ceiling relief above. "I was a passenger, trapped without a way out."

Leah listened carefully before offering her observations.

"Blake, what you encountered was a deficiency in emotional intelligence," Leah said.

Blake grabbed his journal to jot down some notes.

Leah set her wine glass on the immaculate white table.

"It's not just about understanding your own emotions. It's also about reading the room and managing relationships. Both followers and leaders require it. The ship is either sunk or kept afloat by the invisible current."

Blake realized that the meeting was a prime example of bright brains not working together—a case of the "brilliant jerk" phenomenon, in which emotional ignorance produces counterproductive results.

> "A case of the 'brilliant jerk' phenomenon is when emotional ignorance produces counterproductive results."

"High EQ, as it is commonly called, cultivates self-awareness, intellectual humility, and the capacity to be a strong follower," Leah continued, "serves as a defense against bad leadership. Strong followers can correct toxic leaders, while weak followers might support their toxicity. High EQ is critical in the dual roles we all play as leaders and followers."

Leah paused to let Blake catch up.

"When it comes time for us to take the reins, it's not just about persuading people; it's also about modeling the qualities of a capable leader," she added.

Blake nibbled at his salad and glanced up from his journal, thinking about Leah's previous remark.

"I am not sure I have fully processed the duality of being a leader and follower, even though I know we have talked about it."

"Every leader has been a follower at some point." Leah responded. "And EQ is fundamental to both roles. The cornerstones of emotional intelligence (EQ) are self-awareness, self-management, social awareness, and relationship management."

> *"The cornerstones of emotional intelligence (EQ) are self-awareness, self-management, social awareness, and relationship management."*

Leah watched Blake compose a new list in his notebook.

"Our inner compass is self-awareness, our ability to navigate is self-management, our understanding of the seas we sail is social awareness, and our ability to crew our ship is relationship management," Leah said. "A person with a high EQ uses these abilities to lead their team and themselves to success. Similarly, a great follower develops their leadership skills using these same pillars, ensuring that leadership is a positive force rather than a destructive route."

Leah paused thoughtfully as though considering her next words.

"But keep in mind, Blake, that EQ can be used for less honorable goals, just like any other powerful tool. A person with high EQ may utilize their social and self-awareness not only to connect and empathize but also to manipulate. Even though they are able to understand motivations and emotions, they can manipulate them to suit their own agendas."

"Manipulate?" Blake said out loud, recognizing that this word had been used to describe himself over the years. It stung to hear it come from Leah.

"Yes," Leah nodded. "Having a high EQ makes it possible for a person to recognize and impact the emotional currents surrounding them. When used improperly, this term might imply deceiving others and taking advantage of their needs and fears in order to obtain control or authority."

Blake outlined this warning in his journal. The shadowy side of emotional intelligence served as a sobering reminder that honesty is indispensable when walking the path of EQ. Blake determined to exercise his talent to identify and affect emotions in an honorable manner.

Flipping the page in his journal, Blake made a few notes for his follow up email to Erin later that evening.

As the evening wore on, Blake and Leah reflected on the day's events. The emotional undertones of the meeting, the interplay of egos, the unproductive outcomes – it all made sense now. Blake understood that to be effective in both leadership and followership roles, one must master EQ, not just for self-benefit but also for the collective good.

Blake left the restaurant with a fresh understanding and an appreciation for his experience in the boardroom earlier in the day. The journey ahead seemed more straightforward – diving deeper into the realm of EQ and becoming a better leader and follower.

BLAKE'S JOURNAL NOTES TO ERIN

1. *Dual Dynamics:* Understand that EQ is essential in both leading and following. Strong followership cultivates the skills needed for effective leadership.

2. *Pillars of Strength:* Develop the four pillars of EQ: self-awareness, self-management, social awareness, and relationship management—to navigate your dual roles effectively.

3. *Preventing Toxicity:* By enhancing EQ in followership, we not only influence other leaders but also prevent the rise of toxic traits when we assume leadership roles ourselves.

Reflect: *Reflecting on today's meeting, I understand the crucial role EQ plays in leadership and followership. My 'brilliant jerk' tendencies clearly indicate low EQ in play.*

Rethink: *My old way of thinking leads me down a path of manipulation with one end goal: to win at all costs. I need to rethink how I define winning going forward. Not only the end result but how I get there.*

Act: *Moving forward, I need to grow by developing my EQ skills. I'll start by being more aware of my emotions and the emotional cues of others. I will engage in active listening and empathy to better navigate the emotional landscapes of our interactions.*

WEEK FIVE

THE CULTURAL IMPACT

"Culture begins with Story. How we show up, speak up, and sync up tell foundational stories within our culture."

The executive boards convened at an upscale hotel in North Dallas, where the opulence of the setting mirrored both company's stature in the tech world. As the influential members made their entrance, the morning's delicate mist lingered above the lush, meticulously groomed landscapes. The path leading to the hotel, sharp and intentional, was a reflection of the precision and ambition that Blake's firm exemplified within the technology sector.

The air was rich with tension as giants of the industry filled the plush interior. The apprehension surrounding the TechNova merger was palpable as Erin watched Blake open the conversation with his signature passion. He knew the potential for profit was enormous, and the technology was innovative. However, Erin sensed a gap when the conversation turned to integrating strategies.

Erin, familiar with the philosophy of Blake's father, understood that purchasing a business was more than simply taking in its technology—it involved fusing two vital energies. She quietly watched the two CEOs measure each other up, wondering if this meeting would yield a different result than their last gathering.

"If I may," Blake began. "TechNova has unmatched technology, but we're not just here buying patents and algorithms. We are gaining ideas, people, and a culture. The success of this transaction will depend on how we integrate and prioritize these variables, far more than the balance sheets."

The room became quiet. Erin was one of the few who could fully appreciate the significance of this moment. This was not a normal comment coming from the notorious brilliant jerk who led from a self-centered position of ignorance-fueled fear.

"We've seen it in our history," Blake went on. "Our culture and sense of teamwork have been weakened when we placed an undue emphasis on the bottom line. Don't misunderstand, we need to be profitable, but we need to do it right. With TechNova, we can't afford to make that error."

Blake gazed out the window, deep in thought. The other board members slowly nodded, softening the atmosphere a bit. But there was still an air of skepticism that lingered. Was this an attempt to divert their attention? They seemed tentatively optimistic by Blake's remarks that the people and their collective tales were the soul of the company.

The conversation that ensued slowly became directed to culture and human transition, rather than timelines for integration and acquisition strategies.

Blake paced the floor in front of the bay window as the meeting began to wrap up. The lawyers and key staffers from both sides recorded the last few updates from the gathering. Blake began to sense something inside him that felt uncomfortable while leaving him a bit vulnerable.

THE CITY

The trip in his G5 plane back to his office in the city gave Blake time to reflect. Back at his desk, Blake watched the gorgeous skyline rise in the distance while contemplating that a company's culture really is its lifeblood. He felt a sense of satisfaction as he carefully turned the pages in his journal and considered his time in class with Leah earlier this week. Today's understanding served as both a personal turning point and a tactical blueprint for what was to come.

He let himself smile, satisfied with today's outcome, and anticipated his upcoming meeting with Leah to discuss how he was able to apply the lessons from her last lecture in real time. Before the moment slipped away, he found his pen to jot down some notes.

THE CULTURAL NEXUS

Leah's workplace was situated high above the steel and glass jungle of New York City, a peaceful haven amidst the relentless pace of Midtown.

Blake took a seat in the leather chair across from Leah. The sound of the city's pulse faded behind the office's soundproof glass. Leah listened patiently as Blake recounted the story of the last meeting on the pending merger. Below them, the city spread out like a maze of yellow crisscrossing circuits on the back of a mainframe motherboard. After a tough board meeting that tested his cultural intelligence, it felt good to have a sweeping perspective.

"Every decision, every interaction at the board meeting—it's all part of our company's ongoing story," said Blake. "How we show up, not just in our physical presence but in the authenticity of our engagement; how we speak up, our voices reflecting our values; and how we sync up, ensuring our systems, processes, and policies align with our mission—all of this shapes the narrative of our culture."

Leah nodded.

"Blake, you've captured the essence so well. Now, let's explore further. Think about how the board's storyline plays out in this. They are guardians of culture and members of your team, providing guidance and accountability. If they don't realize the story's significance, they run the risk of misaligning your cultural compass."

Leah paused for a moment, reflecting on the occasions when she and her mentor, the Professor, would get together every Saturday morning to talk about the inner workings of culture.

"Blake, you have my undying admiration. As you are aware, a story is the foundation of culture since it shapes our perceptions, guides our actions, and produces results that create new narratives."

Blake nodded, realizing that these were the very words he had heard from his father years ago, only to ignore them out of pride.

"However, when people fail to recognize the significance of those narratives, they don't support culture and allow the brilliant jerk to usurp their authority."

Blake felt her words pierce his soul.

Blake and Leah continued their conversation about the company's cultural fabric as the last of the day's light faded and the Manhattan skyline turned into silhouettes. Leah then guided the topic toward stewardship.

"The purpose of your board," she clarified, "is to make sure the story aligns with the fundamental principles and plan you have outlined, not to control it. Not only do they determine the trends, but they also have to keep an eye on them, comprehend them, and steer them."

Not only do they determine the trends, but they also have to keep an eye on them, comprehend them, and steer them."

> *"The purpose of your board is to make sure the story aligns with the fundamental principles and plan you have outlined, not to control it."*

Blake considered Leah's remarks and realized the nuanced nature of this obligation. The board was tasked with protecting the culture, ensuring it remained strong and aligned with the company's goals, and cultivating it as a valuable corporate asset. He knew he had been less than supportive in the past. He needed to rethink how to direct the conversation at the upcoming board meeting in order to assist the other members in their responsibilities as stewards and monitors of the company's most important story: its culture.

"I can see how our decisions echo through the company's story," he stated. "Our presence, words, systems—they must all be culturally true to who we say we are."

"Yes, as the guardians of the culture, the board plays a vital role," Leah responded. "The goal is to foster and harmonize the story with the organization's core principles rather than to control it."

For the remainder of the evening, Blake and Leah collectively put their heads together and crafted a vision for the board that elevated them beyond their role as mere figureheads to that of stewards of the company's values. With a plan to guarantee that the business's heartbeat matched a meaningful narrative, Blake was in new territory, sensing that his tumultuous relationship with the board could take a turn.

Gripping his journal, Blake jotted down a few notes to help him as he crafted a new experience for his board and, ultimately, for his entire organization

BLAKE'S JOURNAL NOTES TO ERIN

1. *Culture begins with Story:* How we Show Up, Speak Up, and Sync Up tell foundational stories within our culture.
2. *Stories frame our Mindset:* Our stories frame how we think and feel. This includes our values, our beliefs, and our biases, which drive our behavior.
3. *Behavior produces outcomes:* What we do produces our outcomes, which in turn tells a story.

<u>This is culture</u>

[Diagram: a circular flow labeled "culture" with arrows connecting Story → Mindset → Behavior → Outcomes → Story]

Reflect: *It's not just about the systems we integrate but also about the hearts and minds we bring together. Culture is delicate—the essence binds and drives an organization.*

Rethink: *How I continue to advocate for cultural considerations in our decisions needs to be reframed. It's not just about being a successful company; it's about being a significant one.*

Act: *I spoke up today about the importance of culture in our acquisition strategy. It was a risk, but it was necessary.*

WEEK SIX

THE FOLLOWER'S EDGE

"Using your inner strengths—resilience, optimism, hope, and self-efficacy—in your follower position is the essence of Follower Capital."

Gentle morning light permeated the boardroom. Blake was tucked into a high-backed leather chair, and his thoughts were a jumble of introspection and anxiety as he stared blankly out the window. Exhaustion from the recent meetings with the two teams regarding the merger threatened his resilience. Even worse, he had the urge to revert to his old muscle memory. He even reasoned that he was at his best while behaving like the brilliant jerk.

He rocked back and forth slowly in his chair, playing out little scenes in his head of how he could drive this merger home with pure brute force. Embodying the more intelligent but conceited person was not the solution, and his internal conflict simply made him more mentally exhausted. He was grateful he had a class with Leah on the calendar.

THE CLASSROOM

The boulevard was canvassed in a symphony of fall colors under the brushstrokes of an expansive morning sky. The vibrant university grounds were bathed in a warm, rich glow as the morning sun rose gently. Indoors, the normally calm library was a center of intense activity during finals week. Students clustered in every nook and cranny of the old building's wood-paneled reading rooms, trying desperately to stuff what little they had learned throughout the semester into their exhausted brains.

Leah had just wrapped up her office hours, answering last-minute queries from students about her class's impending final, when Blake arrived. his weary eyes brightened amongst the masses of students and their pre-finals energy.

"I'm not sure I could pass your final," Blake said sarcastically. "Especially after this week, which may indicate I'm not the fast learner I thought I was."

"Nonsense!" Leah laughed. "If you set your mind to it, you could easily be the teacher for this class."

"Maybe…if I was still sane enough to apply." Blake's tone had taken on a new weariness.

Leah put her arm around Blake to reassure him.

"Looks like someone is in great need of a scone and hot tea." Leah gestured to the door and led Blake down the marble steps to a quiet coffee shop on the outskirts of campus.

Blake followed obediently, even though a bourbon sounded more appealing. He was relieved, however, by the thought of some more time with Leah.

As soon as they were seated, Blake dug his fork into the blueberry scone while the steam rose from the quirky porcelain cups. His mind wandered to his first meeting with Leah when he was much younger, preparing for college for the first time. The heat from the ginger tea and the sweet taste of the hefty, but airy, pastry evoked a flood of emotions. He leaned into the ladderback chair and shifted his focus to discuss his recent conversation with Erin and the team.

"It sounds like you're facing a real challenge," Leah said. "It's not only the merger; your old inner-struggle has resurfaced."

Blake sipped his drink slowly and nodded.

"I remember some of our early conversations when you were first getting started in business. We discussed the importance of having a strong foundation," Leah recalled, "It was a way to avoid being sucked into the dark side of leadership and followership. I realize that life happens, and success can sometimes be a lousy teacher, but you must continue to strengthen your toxic genius antibodies as you develop and grow in your spheres of influence."

Blake looked thoughtful, fingering the porcelain.

"Blake, we didn't get into this in class, but you must increase your Follower Capital."

Leah paused to search Blake's face.

"How do I do that?" Blake asked.

"Using your inner strengths—***resilience, optimism, hope, and self-efficacy***—in your follower position is the essence of Follower Capital. It involves upholding your moral standards while deftly handling the challenges of both leadership and followership."

Blake leaned forward, knowing he needed this re-direction in order to strengthen his confidence and handle the challenging dynamics ahead.

THE RESILIENCE CAPITAL

"Let's begin by discussing Resilience—the initial facet of Follower Capital," Leah said. "Resilience is about rising above difficulties, not just surviving them. When you engage with others, you attempt to view obstacles as chances to improve and gain new knowledge."

> "Resilience is about rising above difficulties, not just surviving them."

"Resilience," Blake repeated, tapping his fingers on the table. "I like the sound of viewing obstacles as challenges."

"Resilience is an essential tool in this constantly changing journey, where we've navigated the terrains of leadership and followership." Leah went on. "This is about more than just weathering the storm; this is a concept that has been essential to my continued journey to become a person of influence. It is the word that transformed barriers into interesting challenges for me."

Blake quickly produced his journal to capture a few notes for reflection later.

"Our capacity to overcome obstacles and evolve from our experiences is the essence of resilience," Leah continued as she cradled her tea. "Learning from our mistakes and not viewing them as failures is essential to building this capital."

Leah paused for a moment to take a bite of her scone.

"It is revolutionary to view intelligent failures as stepping stones to innovation and growth in an organization—where the stakes are high and the dynamics are complex," Leah said.

Blake continued his notetaking.

"I can understand how this could have an impact," he said.

"This resilience framework must incorporate the concepts of emotional intelligence and mindfulness," Leah added. "By focusing on present-moment awareness, mindfulness enables us to calmly and clearly navigate through the chaos. However, as we've discussed, emotional intelligence gives us the sensitivity to recognize and control our own emotions as well as those of others, particularly in situations where tension is high. When combined, they provide a strong wall that protects us from the demands of our jobs."

Leah leaned forward slightly to pour some more tea for both of them.

"These principles should become your compass as you continue to guide the organization and navigate the complexities of your work. Every failure serves as a teaching moment and every impediment as a chance to fortify this capital. This guarantees that you stay steady, flexible, and constantly evolving as a leader and a follower alike."

THE OPTIMISM CAPITAL

Next, Blake and Leah explored the essence of optimism. The soft murmur of students conversing in the coffee shop was invigorating white noise for a conversation.

"As some would say in ancient times, Blake, optimism is like viewing the world with a Good Eye. It's about seeing possibilities and hope and having a strong spirit despite obstacles," Leah said. "It is more important to keep an optimistic view than to ignore reality."

> "Optimism is like viewing the world with a Good Eye. It's about seeing possibilities and hope and having a strong spirit despite obstacles."

Leah said. "It is more important to keep an optimistic view than to ignore reality."

"So, it's about finding the silver lining in every situation?" Blake observed.

"Exactly. It's about keeping an optimistic attitude and concentrating on what is achievable," Leah smiled. "It's viewing the world through a lens that finds and capitalizes on the positive aspects of every circumstance rather than through rose-colored spectacles. Concentrate on what you can control and accomplish, especially in trying situations with tough people that seemingly come against you."

Leah paused to give Blake time to process the idea.

"Keep in mind that perspective is key to the *Good Eye*. Perspective affects how we view circumstances, difficulties, or even setbacks. Finding the growth, the lessons, and the bright side is what matters. This viewpoint is essential for building resilience and creating an atmosphere that allows followers and leaders to flourish." Leah picked up a chipped, porcelain pot and topped off her cup.

Blake took a moment to skim the page quickly.

"So, building optimism is about creating a culture that encourages growth, innovation, and positive engagement, regardless of the circumstances?" he asked.

"Definitely," Leah replied. "And this is the point at which optimism becomes an effective weapon in our toolbox of leadership and followership. It's about creating a healthy culture that encourages development and constructive involvement even in the most trying circumstances."

THE HOPE CAPITAL

"Now, Remember our previous discussions about hope, Blake?" Leah switched gears. "Dr. Chad Hellman, a colleague of mine, has accomplished amazing work on hope, which is very pertinent in our context. He uses the terms *waypower* and *willpower*, which precisely sums up what you need at this moment."

Blake looked up expectantly.

"Waypower and willpower?"

"Willpower is the mental strength to follow through, and waypower is the ability to see various paths to our goals," Leah explained. "Choosing the appropriate routes in your encounters with others is just as important as perceiving them. This is how you build waypower. And willpower is the ability to stay motivated even when working with someone is difficult."

> "Willpower is the mental strength to follow through, and waypower is the ability to see various paths to our goals,"

Blake immediately understood that the essential component to building Follower Capital was this better comprehension of hope, as seen through the prisms of *waypower* and *willpower*.

THE SELF-EFFICACY CAPITAL

"I know we are covering a lot." Leah leaned in and smiled. "But it is finals week, and this is the time everyone is cramming."

"Like I said," Blake laughed, "I'm pretty sure I couldn't pass your class!"

"Well then, this sounds like a perfect time to talk about self-efficacy," Leah chuckled. "Self-efficacy is about trust in your capability to execute the behaviors necessary to produce specific performance attainments. It's confidence in your ability to influence events that affect your life, and it's control over the way these events are realized."

> *"Self-efficacy is about trust in your capability to execute the behaviors necessary to produce specific performance attainments."*

"So, it's essentially all about my confidence in my skills and decision-making?" Blake felt a familiar tug, reminding him of the insecurities he often masked with his former behaviors.

"Exactly," Leah replied. "And it's important for the capital of your followers. It affects how you approach objectives, assignments, and difficulties. You're more inclined to embark on challenging projects and persevere in the face of difficulty when you have confidence in your own potential."

"Easier said than done." Blake's voice was barely audible as he turned to his journal.

"Perhaps an activity will best illustrate this," Leah offered. "Start with simple, attainable goals. Your confidence in your skills will increase as you get to know them. Think back on your previous accomplishments and keep in mind the abilities that made them possible."

Leah observed Blake write in his journal.

"The act of writing itself is a perfect example of introspection. This is where the 'Reflect' component of the Reflect, Rethink, Act framework becomes crucial, Blake. It's active storytelling, not passive. You are writing the story of your own competency through introspection."

"So, when I reflect, I'm not just looking back—I'm shaping the story of my abilities, which then feeds my self-efficacy?" Blake repeated.

"Exactly," Leah nodded. "Your scriptwriting process transforms obstacles into growth stories. Your confidence grows in these stories, paving the way for further acts and development."

Blake was already aware that his journaling had evolved from a simple habit to a useful tool. This was the one place where he could safely overcome insecurities and build narratives about his power and resiliency, bolstering his confidence with each entry.

"I have an appointment, and we've covered a lot of ground today." Leah stood and grabbed her coat. "I'm going to leave you here to finish your thoughts without any distractions as I can tell this is resonating with you."

Blake barely looked up as Leah quietly slipped through the front door and out into the crisp air.

BLAKE'S JOURNAL NOTES TO ERIN

1. *Journal for Resilience: Strengthen your resilience by recording responses to daily challenges, ensuring you frame each as a learning opportunity.*
2. *Optimism through Visioning: Practice envisioning successful outcomes as progress made in a journal, fostering an optimistic mindset that looks beyond current challenges.*
3. *Pathways and Persistence: By mapping out multiple pathways to your goals and journaling about the persistence needed to walk these paths, you reinforce your "waypower" and "willpower."*
4. *Self-Efficacy Stories: Write narratives of past achievements and skills used to overcome obstacles. It will support cementing your belief in your abilities and enhance self-efficacy.*

Reflect: *In my reflection, I will focus on the instances where I maintained a positive outlook despite difficulties. What was it about these situations that allowed me to stay optimistic? How did my mindset influence the outcome? This introspection will help me understand the power of my perspective and its impact on my journey.*

Rethink: *From my reflections, I need to rethink how I create clearer strategies (Path Insight) for my goals and identify ways to sustain my motivation (Purpose Drive) through the ebbs and flows of workplace dynamics. I'll set specific, measurable steps* to enhance my waypower and willpower, document my progress, and adjust my approach as needed.

Act: Today, I will actively seek out opportunities to demonstrate resilience. Whether it's a challenging conversation with a colleague or a project setback, I will approach it as a chance to strengthen this crucial aspect of my Follower Capital. My actions will be deliberate and aimed at embracing challenges to foster my growth.

WEEK SEVEN

THE SUPPORT STRUCTURE

"Leadership is not about being in charge. It's about taking care of those in your charge."

Blake sat in the conference room, observing the faces of the others on the management team. An undercurrent of unspoken challenges contributed to an atmosphere of tension.

Blake's focus today was diverted as he studied the group, noting that the looks on their faces varied from forced curiosity to open dissatisfaction. He noticed that his teammates appeared to withdraw when his voice rose in decibels. His domineering presence was obviously still telling an old story, impeding their ability to grow and express themselves.

After his conversation with Leah, Blake was clear-headed. He saw the urgent need for a more encouraging setting where each participant could develop and make a meaningful contribution. This called for an environment where everyone, regardless of status, could feel heard and respected.

A young team member caught his eye, and with a cautious glance and a swift nod, they both seemed to be on the same page. Blake knew what had to be done. He had to collaborate with others to create a structure that would allow voices like his to thrive rather than be silenced. This discussion was more than just a project briefing; it was a sobering admission that something needed to change, and Blake felt driven to be the catalyst. It was time to build some Followership Capital, and now he had the playbook to make it happen.

THE LUNCH MEETING

Blake and Leah headed to a small cigar club in the center of Dallas. The morning was cool, and a light wind was blowing through the streets. This was a much-needed time of introspection after class. Blake relaxed into the cozy embrace of the club's deep leather chairs, finding comfort in the peaceful murmur around him. The deep mahogany and dim lighting accented the artwork on the walls. This could not be a more ideal environment for him to explore the intricacies he had been thinking about between leadership and followership.

As Blake settled in, Leah picked up the small menu to look at the lunch choices.

"I should have guessed you would have picked this location sooner or later, " she said with a hint of jest in her voice. "Don't be surprised if I tell you this is not my first time here," she added with a wink.

Blake's face showed a hint of intrigue.

"Do tell," he inquired as a server approached to take their drink order.

"Maybe later," she replied, as she ordered an extra dirty martini. "So, what's on your mind that you brought me to your club for our talk?" she deflected, beating Blake at his own game.

"Do I run the risk of staying an idiosyncratic, brilliant jerk if I ignore my capacity for leadership? Talented but devoid of the very traits that define a truly effective leader?" Blake asked abruptly. "How's that for diving right in?"

Leah smiled appreciably, her face gradually growing serious.

"That's a perceptive question, my friend," Leah said. "Leaders who disregard followership teachings frequently miss opportunities to grow in empathy, teamwork, and appreciation of different viewpoints. They might succeed in the short run, but always at the expense of cohesiveness and long-term faith in the team."

This insight highlighted the need to maintain a healthy balance between followership abilities and leadership prowess—an issue Blake recognized he needed to explore. He also knew if he delved deeper, he ran a great risk of uncovering a side of himself that was potentially darker than he was willing to admit.

The server returned, and Blake waited for her to set down their drinks before probing Leah with a follow-up question. He took a small sip of the chilled bourbon.

"How does a leader protect against that?"

Leah sensed his vulnerability.

"Just as an organization has a board of directors, individuals should consider forming a personal board, as well. A personal board of directors is more than just a collection of advisors. It's a dynamic framework that changes as you do."

"I think I'm tapped out with the current board I have," Blake said sarcastically. "Isn't there a saying about too many cooks in the kitchen?"

"Not when they are experienced chefs," Leah shot back. "Imagine receiving insight and guidance from someone who has already experienced your road. Then, there's a peer who offers support and wisdom because they are aware of your present challenges and victories. Remember the person you're mentoring as well; their new insights might serve as a helpful reminder of your influence and the wider picture."

"It does sound like having a personal sounding board for every aspect of my journey," Blake said, imagining familiar faces in each of these roles.

"Exactly," Leah nodded. "Think of the levels of support provided by collaborators, coaches, and counselors in addition to this board. Each contributes uniquely to your development by providing various forms of advice and opportunity."

Thinking of this framework as a complex scaffold-like support system, Blake saw its potential. Not only could he improve his leadership, but also his followership would be enhanced. He believed that this would help him manage the complicated relationships he encountered and promote a more all-encompassing strategy for his journey forward. Reaching into his backpack, he produced his journal for a few quick notes.

The concept of a personal board of directors was more than appealing—especially having a network of people who could provide counsel and a variety of viewpoints.

He opened his journal and thought about who his board members would be. In addition, he was surprised by the relational subtlety in becoming a leader and a follower. It took more than simple leadership to be an effective follower. He recognized he would need to develop these abilities to keep the brilliant jerk at bay. Blake now understood that the real secret is to always be learning and adapting.

BLAKE'S JOURNAL NOTES TO ERIN

1. *Personal Board of Directors: Cultivate a diverse personal board, including someone ahead of you in your career, someone in the same season as you, and someone you are bringing along. This board provides varied insights, enriching your development as both a leader and a follower.*

2. *Balance in Leadership and Followership: Embrace the interconnectedness of leadership and followership. Develop followership skills—like empathy and collaboration—to enhance your leadership and avoid the "brilliant jerk" phenomenon.*

3. *Continuous Learning and Adaptation: Regularly assess and refine your approach to both roles. Stay open to feedback and new perspectives, ensuring a dynamic and effective leadership-followership balance.*

Reflect: *The balance between leadership and followership is delicate and intertwined. The discussion made me realize the risk of neglecting followership skills and remaining the "brilliant jerk." It's a pitfall I'm now more aware of and determined to avoid.*

Rethink: *I don't have to have all the answers all the time. I'll focus on fostering these relationships and ensuring I'm as effective in my followership as I am in my leadership. It's a continuous journey of learning, growth and adaptation.*

Act: *Today, in Dallas, Leah introduced me to the idea of a personal board of directors. It's a concept that adds depth to my understanding of leadership support systems. I'm planning to identify and reach out to potential board members.*

WEEK EIGHT

THE MIRROR OF PROFESSIONALISM

"Strategic followership is about aligning your efforts with the broader goals of the organization, not just following orders."

The open office plan at WatNex was Blake's vision—a collaborative space intended to foster creativity and unity. Once fully embracing the power of collaboration, his exacting demeanor overshadowed his intellect, exposing all to the toxic overflow of a brilliant jerk. His time with Leah had slowly softened his edge as he navigated his new path; however, despite the progress made, he remained a work in progress. Today, the dissonance was real. The team was witness to his ongoing transformation as he navigated the fine line between assertiveness and respect.

With her keen eye for the undercurrents of office dynamics, Erin observed Blake pacing the floor with a phone to his ear. His voice was elevated while he covered more ground than a basketball player on a fast break. His furrowed brow deepened with the heated conversation—one probably not suited for an audience. His tone was exceedingly sharp.

"I understand the client's perspective is paramount, and normally, that would be our priority. But today, *our* expertise trumps their desires. Period. End of discussion."

His words, though assertive, didn't entirely communicate the respect he'd been cultivating with his team.

In a moment, the atmosphere in the office shifted, the energy waning as the team absorbed Blake's public conversation. There was a collective silence for reflection, as if the office itself held its breath.

Erin scanned the room, noting the momentary lull in their collective rhythm.

New to the ebb and flow of WatNex's culture, a new hire shifted uncomfortably in the uncommon quiet. She nervously glanced toward Erin who calmly met her gaze, offering silent reassurance by means of a gentle smile and a nod.

As evidenced by this misstep, it was clear Blake was still learning to thread the needle between his brilliant jerk self and the leader he aimed to be. His progress with Leah, a testament to his efforts, hadn't been undone by this momentary lapse. But a story had just been told that could impede the progress of the office culture.

Blake's call ended with audible contact between his phone and the conference room table. The employees in the room were startled and gingerly retreated. Blake, feeling the weight of scrutiny, briskly walked away to avoid further confrontation.

Erin approached with a composed air of someone familiar with the tides of change. Blake looked troubled, and Erin wondered if it was indicative of a deep frustration with himself.

"Blake, might we talk? Privately?" she said in an inviting tone.

He nodded as the stern lines of his face softened into something more reflective. He followed Erin to a space where they could converse privately.

The day hadn't started off this way. Blake's problem-solving abilities were unmatched, and his ideas had propelled WatNex to unprecedented heights over the last 15 years. This morning was a perfect illustration. The group gathered around him as he skillfully worked his way through an intricate algorithm that had baffled them for weeks. His thoughts were laser-focused as his fingers danced across the keyboard. The team's stunned reaction was evidence of his expert skill.

But when the call came, a wave of conceit eclipsed his intelligence. The brilliant jerk, albeit a toned-down version, stepped into the light and was exposed once more.

When Erin shut the door, the quiet meeting room felt tense. Erin took a seat across from Blake, who was still shaking off his earlier moment—one he was beginning to recognize after the fact. Blake appeared both expectant and uneasy.

"Blake, let's talk about the story that just unfolded. It wasn't just about a tough decision or the pressure of the deal we are working to close," Erin said insightfully. "It was about professionalism, which may seem more basic but is ten times as important."

Blake shifted uneasily, his customary assurance faltering beneath Erin's unwavering gaze.

"I think you are over-exaggerating, Erin. Besides, the pressure is just…"

Erin stopped him abruptly with a raised hand.

"First of all, Blake, I'm not exaggerating. It's not only about managing pressure. Being professional is about the image we present of ourselves, particularly when things get tight. It concerns the narrative of our proficiency, behavior, and personality."

THE COMPETENCE FACTOR

"Blake, how would you define competence?" She allowed him time to think through her question.

"It's frequently interpreted as an indicator of your depth of knowledge and innate abilities," she said. "However, what does it actually mean to use that skill when under duress?"

Blake shifted in his chair.

"Imagine you're faced with a difficult decision and the ethical path isn't the easiest one," Erin said. "What part does competence play in the decision you make?"

Blake considered Erin's inquiry. He nodded slowly, recognizing that competence was a dynamic force rather than merely a static asset.

"It's...it's about how reliably I can bring those skills to bear when it counts, isn't it?" His tone was contemplative.

"Yes," Erin replied.

"Competence is the capacity to use those abilities to negotiate ambiguity and complexity and to stick to your values even when temptation calls for taking short cuts. It's all about being the professional you can always rely on, especially in situations where the stakes are high and the decisions are difficult."

> *"Competence is the capacity to use those abilities to negotiate ambiguity and complexity and to stick to your values even when temptation calls for taking short cuts."*

With a gentle but forceful invitation to investigate, Erin leaned in.

"Blake, let's pause to think for a while. How can we continue to develop in our roles? How can we be certain that we are capable in those roles today, tomorrow, and beyond? Isn't the goal of continuous learning more than knowledge acquisition? It concerns flexibility and our readiness to relearn as we go through our personal and professional trajectories."

"So, it's an ongoing process?" Blake commented.

"Exactly." Erin fixed her gaze on his. "And both leadership and followership revolve around this process. It involves co-creating an organizational culture in which we all contribute to a common understanding that, in turn, benefits us all as leaders, followers, instructors, and students."

Her remarks mirrored his previous conversations with Leah. The notion that leadership was a collaborative dance rather than a solitary endeavor with followership was appealing. He had learned from Leah that The Follower Effect was about embodying humility and excitement in equal measure—standing boldly in what you know while keeping open to learning what you don't.

> *"The Follower Effect was about embodying humility and excitement in equal measure—standing boldly in what you know while keeping open to learning what you don't."*

"This shared journey of continuous learning forges our team's deeper connections," Erin stated. "It involves coordinating our abilities and group objectives to make sure that we are all contributing to a task bigger than ourselves.

"Unlike today," Blake said, under his breath.

"Listen, as you travel this path, Blake, both your leadership and learning roles are crucial. It's about striking a balance between collaborative followership and directive leadership, making space for discussion and the flow of knowledge that empowers each team member."

Blake remained contemplative, listening to Erin.

"Think of our company culture as a tapestry of stories. Every strand tells a story of choices, victories, and lessons discovered. Continuous learning is one of these vivid threads that colors our acts and our legacy."

Blake was intrigued by the allegory.

"So, our growth as leaders and followers…it's a story that never ends?"

"Exactly," Erin answered. "Furthermore, these narratives cover more ground than just individual successes. They speak to our journey as a group about how we accept learning as leaders and how we add to that knowledge as followers. It's about the narratives we create together, the lessons we learn from each other, and our common experiences."

He remembered the many stories they had read—the tales of resiliency that exemplified their grit, the epics of teamwork that highlighted their oneness, and the reflective narratives that revealed their introspection.

"Our stories are dynamic and always changing as we overcome obstacles and achieve victories. We are not just a part of the culture we teach, lead, and follow. We are its creators," Erin said. "We tell stories all the time when we Sync Up, Show Up, and Speak Up."

He smiled in spite of himself, realizing that most of these concepts that Erin was addressing came through Leah by way of his father. Thinking of his father, these ideas struck a deep chord. Each page served as a monument to their development and the enduring force of the stories they told. They were all authors in their own right, writing the unfolding chapters of their organization's journey.

Blake, who was normally eager to express his ideas, was suddenly thoughtful and realized his previous experience with the team would need to be interpreted with a level of humility in order to tell a different story.

THE CONDUCT FACTOR

"After thinking about the story we weave with our ongoing learning," Erin continued, "let's pivot to another aspect that's just as critical—conduct."

Her tone suggested that they were moving to a more concrete part of their conversation—the part that pertained to his behavior today.

"The core of our professional story is conduct. The deeds in the Show Up story speak louder than any words we may write."

Blake listened closely, his previously defensive stance softening.

"Blake, never forget that every interaction and choice you make reveals something about who you are. These tales are also remembered. They linger in the hallways, influencing how people see us and, in the end, defining the legacy we leave behind."

Erin emphasized the interplay of respect, accountability, and responsibility—each an important chapter in the great tale of an organization—drawing on the thoughts of professionalism.

"You are the one who sets the pace and the example that others follow with your conduct. You don't simply tell the tale of professionalism; you live it when you treat your coworkers with respect, accept accountability for your actions, and accept responsibility for the results."

Erin timed her next thoughts carefully.

"Behavior, Blake, embodies our twofold roles as leaders and followers." She raised her hands to visually cover both domains. "It's about how our behavior in one role reflects and influences the other." She leveraged a stern shake of each hand when saying "one" and "other."

"Our behavior doesn't happen in a vacuum," Erin continued. "It ripples throughout our company, affecting the confidence of our colleagues, the morale of our team, and our overall path. This is the essence of the Follower Effect—where we not only lead by example but also FOLLOW by example—where our conduct as followers can inspire leadership in others and vice versa. It creates a precedent when you, as a leader, act with respect. It promotes a culture in which every participant, even as a follower, feels appreciated and heard. This, in turn, creates an atmosphere that is conducive to creativity and teamwork."

> "This is the essence of the Follower Effect—where we not only lead by example but also FOLLOW by example—where our conduct as followers can inspire leadership in others and vice versa."

She paused to assess his willingness to continue. He was slowly nodding, taking it all in.

"Furthermore," Erin pressed on, "behavior serves as a link between followership and leadership. This is the point at which the behavior and the values of professionalism—respect, accountability, and responsibility—intersect. Your actions in times of stress, uncertainty, success, and failure tell the unspoken tale of your character as a leader and a follower."

Erin drove her point home.

"Blake, behavior counts. It is contagious and the outward manifestation of our inner principles. Good behavior breeds more good behavior, which spreads across the entire organization. The heart of the Follower Effect is this: we not only provide an example for others to follow, but we also follow our own. In other words, our actions as followers can encourage others to take on leadership roles and vice versa. We all take on the role of stewards of the culture we want to foster in this way."

THE CHARACTER FACTOR

"We've established that our conduct as leaders and followers sets a standard in our journey through the Follower Effect," Erin said. "Let's now discuss character, which is the cornerstone of that ideal. When there are no norms to moor us, it's the compass that leads us through the obscurity."

"I'm thinking we are considering my character today?" Blake looked off into the distance, deep in thought.

"Yes and no. Today is just one aspect and example of your character. Character is about the truth we embody when no one is watching. It's the integrity that endures in the face of pressure, the honesty we maintain in every transaction, and the justice we incorporate into every choice."

> *"Character is about the truth we embody when no one is watching. It's the integrity that endures in the face of pressure, the honesty we maintain in every transaction, and the justice we incorporate into every choice."*

Leaning forward, she looked into Blake's eyes.

"Our character is demonstrated by our leadership style and our teamwork style. Furthermore, our character is the recurring thread in every chapter of our organization's grand tale, influencing our culture, brand, and legacy."

Erin spoke to Blake about leadership basics with confidence, referencing a colleague of Leah's research. She explained that integrity, responsibility, forgiveness, and compassion are not just innate traits. They are also crucial skills that can be developed to enhance an individual's character and achieve solid business outcomes.

"Those sound more like a list of elementary virtues than pathways to business outcomes," Blake said.

"I can see how that would be your immediate reaction, but consider integrity," Erin continued. "Being ethical, real, and consistent in all of your actions and choices is important. Trust is the currency of both leadership and followership, and it is imperative that this be maintained."

She spoke gingerly.

"Then let's re-evaluate how we perceive accountability and responsibility. Accountability is not about checking boxes or playing a part; it's about accepting the results of our actions, regardless of their nature. Responsibility extends beyond mere accountability. It's about owning our actions and consciously directing the story with the choices we make. We use the pen of responsibility to create our story, whether we are in the spotlight as leaders or in the supporting position as followers. And while we do that, we have to be prepared to hold that pen tightly and write our victories and lessons learned with the same openness and dedication."

"Why do I sense there is still more to this explanation?" Blake searched Erin's face.

Erin's tone took on more compassion as she prepared to address the subject of forgiveness.

"Forgiveness is a multifaceted gem in the crown of leadership and followership," she said. "It's about accepting ourselves when we make errors and realizing that creativity frequently emerges from the ashes of previous failures. By releasing oneself from the constraints of perfectionism, self-forgiveness enables us to take chances and pursue creativity."

Then she turned her attention outward.

"When we forgive, we're fostering connection rather than merely patching up a rift. It's about realizing that everyone is on a unique path of personal development. The key to bridging the divide between cooperation and conflict is forgiveness. Moving ahead together and learning from the error is more important than forgetting the mistake. This collective act of forgiving within a team serves as the foundation for trust and the impetus for cohesive advancement. Without fear or anger, it enables us to fully utilize the range of our skills as a group, which leads to innovation, connection, and eventually success."

"That is a lot to take in," Blake said. "And not easy to apply either."

"That's why I saved compassion for last," Erin said. "Compassion is the capacity to comprehend the viewpoints and difficulties of others, creating a nurturing atmosphere that improves well-being among all. The duality of leadership and followership is operational, but these character traits make it transformative, opening the door to an ethically successful culture of excellence."

She noticed Blake take out his journal.

"By doing this, we fortify not just our abilities but also our character. We develop into followers who can lead and leaders worthy of being followed."

Erin glanced over at Blake who had started writing in his journal.

"And these also apply to how you treat yourself, Blake. If you offer compassion to yourself first, you will be filled up to offer it to those around you."

She stood up to leave.

"I look forward to receiving your notes."

BLAKE'S JOURNAL NOTES TO ERIN

1. *Reflection on Conduct: Today was a stark reminder that my actions profoundly impact our team's spirit. I've learned that true competence is about consistently applying my skills and knowledge, especially under pressure, to uphold our collective narrative of professionalism. My resolve is to embody the principles of accountability and respect, regardless of stressors, maintaining the positive image I aim to project.*

2. *Character as a Compass: Acknowledging my lapse in professionalism, I understand character isn't just an internal compass; it's an observable beacon that guides others. Traits like integrity, responsibility, and compassion are not static—they evolve through our actions and decisions. I commit to demonstrating these traits through my behavior, recognizing that they are as important in defining competence as my technical skills.*

3. *Professional Growth and Adaptability: I am reminded that growth is an ever-present process, especially in leadership. Embracing adaptability and continuous learning is vital. Reflecting on today's shortfall, I am motivated to fortify my resilience and optimistic outlook, recognizing that my narrative is not defined by one setback but by the ongoing journey of personal and professional evolution.*

Reflect: This conversation highlighted the strength found in self-forgiveness and the power it unleashes for personal and team innovation. *It also reminded me of the importance of extending forgiveness to others, which is fundamental in building strong, cohesive bonds.*

Rethink: *Today's insights, while difficult to hear, have added a new dimension to my leadership and followership growth. Recognizing the role of forgiveness in professional settings has taught me that our greatest breakthroughs often follow our biggest mistakes, provided we have the courage to forgive and forge ahead.*

Act: *Today's dialogue about the intricacies of forgiveness in our professional conduct was enlightening. By fostering a forgiving mindset, I've learned to encourage innovation and connection within my team, allowing us all to move past errors toward collective achievement.*

WEEK NINE

THE PARADOX OF BEING VERSES HAVING

"True power comes from humility and the willingness to learn from others, regardless of their position."

The last college student left, leaving just Leah and Blake in the empty classroom.

"Blake, what were your thoughts on class today?" Leah asked. "I've been eager to catch up."

Leah's smile warmed the room and Blake suspected that Leah had most likely received a call from Erin recapping the events of last week.

Leah noticed his hesitation.

"I have come to realize that there are always two sides to every story, and the majority of the time, the middle is where the solution lies," Leah nudged. "May I ask how you are feeling about last week?"

Blake sat down across from Leah, his hands clenching and releasing as he tried to gather his thoughts.

"It was frustrating, humiliating, and illuminating all at once. I had no idea how difficult this journey could be," Blake responded.

Leah nodded.

"I never said it would be easy. What I did say is that if you put in the work, it would be rewarding."

"And I'm trusting that will be the outcome," Blake said. "At the time, though, it felt like I was on a tightrope with no net or balancing pole."

"Blake, that's the core of being a follower. The Follower Effect involves navigating your influence in any direction, upward, peer-to-peer, or downstream.

It all comes down to influence, no matter which way it goes."

Blake leaned closer. "I think I'm beginning to comprehend the 'follower impact' that you speak of, Leah. However, I still have a lot to learn."

Blake unclasped his hands.

"I guess that's why I'm still in the classroom and not the boardroom today. This is where the conflict between 'being' versus 'having' arises. Leaders and followers are more than just repositories of information. They are a transformative catalyst and a light of impact." Blake added thoughtfully. "So it goes beyond what I possess, such as my knowledge or talents?"

> "Leaders and followers are more than just repositories of information. They are a transformative catalyst and a light of impact."

Blake added thoughtfully. "So it goes beyond what I possess, such as my knowledge or talents?"

"Exactly," Leah replied. "What really distinguishes your journey as a leader and follower is who you are—your demeanor, your approach, your empathy, and your patience. Being the person who aids in the discovery of the solutions is more important than possessing all the answers."

"I believe I'm prepared for the next step, Leah. Even though this journey has become intensely personal for me, too, I think I am prepared to go even deeper." Blake resembled a soldier in a rare moment of surrender.

"Let's talk about the power of being in leadership," Leah said as she fixed her gaze on Blake.

THE DARK SIDE OF HAVING

"You know, Blake, most commonly in our society, success is determined by our possessions—wealth, power, and position. While these are not always harmful, they can be deceptive when used as the only measures of achievement."

Blake nodded.

"Most of my colleagues frame their posture around those things for sure. It's like a subtle race to the top—the more horsepower the better," Blake responded.

"Unfortunately, yes," Leah went on. "Here's the catch, though. One might become self-centered when the desire of possessing something—be it money, position, or power—becomes their only goal in life. This is the point at which the archetype of the 'brilliant jerk' emerges. Brilliant jerks are individuals who have conventional success but are devoid of empathy, genuineness, or the capacity to establish meaningful connections with others."

"I think we've all experienced that at one time or another," Blake said, surprised by his personal conviction.

"Blake, when we obsess over our own interests, we run a serious risk. It provides access to what psychologists refer to as the 'dark triad' of followership and leadership."

The phrase "dark triad," interested Blake. He pulled out his journal.

"The dark triad?" he inquired.

"It's a psychological notion that refers to three personality traits: psychopathy, Machiavellianism, and narcissism," Leah responded. "These characteristics can be seen in leaders or even followers who excessively prioritize their own needs and feelings over those of others. A haughty sense of self-importance is the result of narcissism, manipulation and exploitation are the result of Machiavellian behavior, and a lack of empathy and regret is the result of psychopathy."

It wasn't difficult for Blake to make connections between so many of the earlier exchanges with his team and Erin.

"So, the shadowy side of leadership and followership is this dark triad?" Blake mused while writing.

"That's right," Leah confirmed. "It is the very opposite of the sincere, customer-focused strategy we have been talking about. Those who fit into this dark triad as leaders or followers are driven by their inner brilliant jerk. Even if they may be successful in traditional measures, their success is frequently realized at the expense of others. Worse, it is based on deceit or manipulation and lacks genuine empathy or connection. This is the reason it's so important to comprehend how to reconcile 'having' with 'being.' It serves as a defense against slipping into these harmful habits. Empathy, honesty, and sincerity are qualities that true leaders and followers emphasize. We also need to use our influence for the benefit of society as a whole rather than just ourselves."

Blake nodded, both relieved and uncomfortable at the implication of these words.

"So, it's a warning story about the perils of losing sight of who we are as we chase our desires?" he questioned, putting down his pen.

"That's right," Leah said. "And it emphasizes the significance of our path in leadership and followership—to be self-aware, mindful, and constantly strive to serve others as much as we seek to achieve our own goals."

THE POWER OF DISCERNMENT

Blake slowly leaned back onto the classroom chair, feeling like the student called to task by the teacher.

"Leah, some may argue that your strategy is a little too utopian. What about the hard reality of being a leader? The mindset of 'kill or be killed,' which some people think is essential for success?" Blake was thinking about his last several years leading in the global marketplace.

"You make a valid point, Blake. It's true that the world may be harsh, and being a leader frequently means making harsh choices. But being strong doesn't have to mean sacrificing your humanity, integrity, or even empathy. The key to being a true leader and follower is facing obstacles head-on and staying true to your principles."

Leah moved to sit on a chair beside Blake.

"Being tough doesn't always translate into violence or harshness. It may have to do with perseverance and sticking up for what's right in the face of difficulty. It involves leading with a feeling of responsibility and having the guts to make difficult choices while also taking into account how those choices will affect other people."

"You're saying that having compassion and being tough doesn't have to conflict with each other?" Blake was having trouble picturing that dynamic.

"True leadership is complex," Leah answered. "It's about striking a balance between empathy and assertiveness. While there may be short-term benefits to the 'kill or be killed' mentality, it frequently results in long-term issues—including low morale, a toxic culture, and a lack of trust. Building relationships, trust, and a culture where people feel appreciated and inspired are all essential components of sustainable leadership.

"Sometimes, that just seems impossible—like the true definition of pie in the sky." Blake looked resigned.

"Effective followership makes this possible," Leah said. "Keep in mind that being a leader is not the only aspect of it. It concerns the culture the leaders foster, the people they lead, and the legacy they leave behind. A leader who lacks empathy and is solely capable of winning physical battles may lose the war in terms of long-term contentment and success."

Blake nodded, the puzzle pieces shifting resolutely.

"I'm thinking that the key to unlocking this possibility is to be firm but fair, powerful but kind, behaving with respect for both ourselves and other people."

Leah grinned, appreciative of Blake's comprehension.

"That's right. That's what makes a leader effective. It's not a *compromise* between kindness and toughness. It's about *possessing* the discernment to know which to be when."

"There's that word again—possession," Blake commented.

"Yes. Discernment is truly a leader's most valuable possession."

THE POWER OF BEING

"So, this discernment definitely seems to be tied to my self-awareness, right?" Blake remarked while he wrote. "However, it appears that success is equally significant."

"It is," Leah concurred. "But you shouldn't let it control you. This is the point at which the idea of 'being' is relevant. It's about being something greater than the sum total of your belongings or titles. It all boils down to serving people and being real, open, and authentically vulnerable."

"Greater than the sum total of your titles?" Blake asked.

"Consider Jesus, for example. His goal in life was not to amass fortune or prestige. It was about serving others, being loving and compassionate, and imparting knowledge. Not because of his possessions but rather because of his character and selfless way of living, he was a leader."

"So, we can lead more effectively if we focus on being who we are—on our qualities, character, and how we treat others?"

"Yes," Leah replied. "It's about rewriting the history of conventional leadership. We satisfy our own deepest aspirations when we are obedient followers who put others' needs first and assist them in reaching their objectives. Essentially, we get what we want while empowering others. The core of authentic leadership and followership is this dichotomy."

Blake stood up to stretch his stiff legs.

"So, my journey is less about what I can amass and more about who I am as a person during the process?"

"That's right." Leah grinned, standing and gathering her things. "It's about showcasing the power of being—your sincerity, your compassion, and your readiness to show vulnerability. These are the attributes that will turn you into an exceptional leader as well as an effective follower."

BLAKE'S JOURNAL NOTES TO ERIN

1. *Balancing Toughness and Compassion:* Understand that being tough in leadership does not exclude compassion and empathy. It's about making difficult decisions while being mindful of their impact on others.
2. *Cultivating Sustainable Leadership:* Focus on building relationships and trust and nurturing a culture where everyone feels valued. This approach ensures long-term success over short-term gains.
3. *Legacy of Leadership:* Always be mindful of the legacy you leave as a leader. True success is measured both in achievements and the positive impact on people and the culture nurtured.

Reflect: Today's conversation with Leah opened my eyes to the balance between toughness and compassion in leadership. It's a reminder that my actions as a leader should be strong but also empathetic, taking into account the well-being of others.

Rethink: I've come to realize that short-term gains achieved through a "kill or be killed" mentality can lead to long-term issues like mistrust and low morale. Sustainable leadership, on the other hand, is about fostering a supportive and trusting environment.

Act: It would seem I have a choice to make…

THE CATALYST OF CHANGE

"Change is not just a goal or a destination but a process of continuous transformation that requires persistent effort and adaptation."

Blake stood alone in his large, well-organized office, staring out the window. The skyline shimmered with the last of the sunset—the unrelenting buzz of the city receding into the distance. His thoughts, which were generally focused on plans and results, were consumed by Erin's resolute challenge: "We need to see the change in you."

His gaze shifted indoors and rested on the wood-framed picture sitting on his desk—a rare, intimate image of him with his father. It was taken during a fishing trip that seemed like a lifetime ago—a trip that was more about companionship than business. Blake had always looked up to his father. A man of few words, his father's impactful presence embodied fortitude and perseverance.

Blake picked up the photo. The fishing trip was one of the few opportunities that provided Blake and his father alone time together. Blake reflected on that moment along peaceful Willow Creek, the secret location known by only a few. He remembered the water's surface shimmering in the early morning light as Willow Creek came to life, heralding a day filled with the peaceful excitement of fly fishing. Blake and his father had waded into the cool, running waters with their fly rods in hand. The tall willows encircling the creek created a remote haven where the sounds of the outside world vanished, leaving just the rush of the river's flow and the swishing of the fishing line.

An expert fly fisherman, his father showed him how to throw with a beautiful arc, the line falling almost silently across the surface of the river until it rested with hardly a ripple.

"It's not just about catching fish," his father had said, his gaze moving with the line as it drifted downstream. "Knowing the fish, the water, and yourself is key. It involves precision, patience, and the serenity that results from being totally present in the moment."

As they continued to cast their lines into the water, the Professor spoke, his voice calm and steady against the background of the flowing river.

"Blake, do you see how the water navigates the rocks, never stopping, always finding a way through or around the obstacles it encounters?"

Blake nodded, watching the water's effortless journey downstream.

"That's much like how we should navigate our interactions with others," the Professor continued, his eyes fixed on the line he had cast. "You'll meet people who seem like obstacles in your path. It's easy to feel contempt for those who don't see the world as we do and who challenge us. But contempt blocks us, like a dam in the river, preventing understanding and growth."

Blake, his attention split between his father's words and the line in the water, didn't fully grasp the depth of the lesson being offered.

But the Professor, patient as always, pressed on.

"True strength, Blake, lies in our ability to understand, empathize, and find a way to move forward together. Much like the river, we must learn to navigate our differences and respect the flow of ideas and emotions without letting them flood our sense of self or drown our capacity for compassion."

Blake pondered this memory and set the photo back on his desk, his father's words feeding his mind. He remembered that he came to the realization that the main benefit of fly fishing was not the quantity of fish caught. Instead, it was the peace of mind and the relationships it cultivated—not just with his father but also with nature as they released their catches.

Blake realized his father had been teaching him the early lessons of followership as they stood waist-deep in Willow Creek. Fly fishing with the man who first personified the epitome of calm, strength, and wisdom, Blake could now see how his father, the Professor, was setting him on his own path of personal development.

THE REMNANT OF THE PAST

Blake felt the weight of unspoken words and unresolved admiration flood his mind. At that moment, the room's silence was broken by the echo of his father's voice—a final comment he had made—which echoed gruff with time and emotion.

"Remember, Son, the true measure of a man is not how he leads but how he lifts those around him."

"The true measure of a man is not how he leads but how he lifts those around him."

While the words had been meant to serve as direction, Blake had long since buried them beneath the honors and accomplishments he believed to be signs of success. Standing before the sprawling city below, his father's final words now resurfaced with an immediacy and clarity that caught him off guard.

THE SILENT MOMENT

Blake sat down and considered his team's difficult moments, Erin's unwavering challenge, and his developing awareness of the gap between his behavior and the principles his father had taught. He knew he had to face the contradiction of the guy he wanted to be and the leader he had become. This was his moment of reckoning—a profound awareness that his intelligence, devoid of compassion and understanding, had kept him apart from the people he aimed to guide.

THE CHOICE

As the evening grew darker, Blake made a decision. It was time to close the gap between his goals and deeds and live up to the values his father had instilled in him—the values both Leah and Erin had been nobly trying to coax out of him. It was time to stop dictating respect and start encouraging it. It was time to start exercising authority over others in order to promote teamwork.

Blake touched the picture resolutely one last time. The road ahead would demand humility, bravery, and an openness to change—not only for WatNex's benefit but also for his own development as a leader, follower, and person.

Blake knew that every resolution would be tested and that the real test of his determination would come the moment he stepped in the boardroom. In this silent moment of contemplation, he had discovered his agent of change.

THE REFLECTION

WatNex's boardroom was buzzing with anticipation as the sun descended below the horizon, bathing the busy city in a golden glow. There was an obvious feeling of nervous excitement as Erin and Blake stood in front of the assembled crew. It was as if everyone sensed that an important turning point in their journey—one filled with lessons and obstacles—was about to occur.

THE PROPOSAL

Erin opened the conversation with the calm assurance of someone who had sailed through turbulent times of transition.

"We're not just wrapping up a merger today," she said, her voice heavy with the collective experience of them both. "We're celebrating the evolution of our leadership and followership dynamics."

Standing in front of his colleagues, Blake viewed them with the new eyes of a changed man—his slow transformation from a "brilliant jerk" to a thoughtful leader replete with moments of epiphany and resistance.

With a humble voice, Blake addressed the room. "Recently, I've embarked upon a personal journey—one that was also intended to impact all of those who surround me. During this season, I've learned that brilliance without empathy is merely arrogance. We are stronger when we work together, listen to each other, and develop as a team rather than when we dictate."

> "Brilliance without empathy is merely arrogance."

The room was silent, absorbing Blake's change in posture with both skepticism and hope.

"I have come to the realization that the ability to adapt, sympathize, and come together in pursuit of a common objective is the genuine core of leadership and followership."

No one could deny that Blake's manner had gradually changed. It was a slow awakening rather than an abrupt metamorphosis—as though the hard edges of his former posture were being rounded like the steady course of a creek flowing over rock. There was hope in the air—hope that WatNex's cultural climate could experience a renewal.

Much like the arrival of spring after an especially hard winter, team members began to detect the thaw of their customary caution around Blake's strong leadership style. Slowly, tentative talks started to surface, gauging the waters in this unfamiliar setting. Once guarded like trade secrets under layers of protective self-interest, their ideas could now be discussed with cautious optimism. The initial skepticism began to thaw, too, as a result of Blake's transparent acknowledgment of his shortcomings. As Leah had said, it was his humility that became the first step in cultivating a growing trust.

Projects that were formerly approval battlegrounds were now approached cooperatively. There was a noticeable change in the air in the WatNex hallways—a cautious optimism. Once thought to be unachievable, this cooperation would now be the team's main motivator.

But everyone was also aware that this was just the start. As Leah also said, culture is not changed by one action but rather by repeated intentional stories. Blake and the team's journey was still in the early phases—the beginning of a new story. The full blossom of transformation, promise, and struggle awaited them as they explored this new terrain together.

THE THOUGHTS

As Blake reflected on the journey, he found that his thoughts held command over the room.

"Our path was illuminated by the challenges we faced," he said, casting a glance over the group. "And it was through navigating these challenges that we discovered our collective strength. If I haven't said this enough before, thank you for all you have contributed to both my journey and the journey of this team."

Instead of feeling the compulsion to reach a formal conclusion, the gathering finished with an open-ended pledge to continue developing, learning, and collaborating. That pledge rested on the strength of Blake's sincere apology.

The team departed as the sun dipped below the horizon. The gentle glow in the boardroom symbolized the start of a new chapter in the WatNex narrative—one of change, resiliency, and the strength of group leadership.

When Blake walked back into his office, Leah and Erin were waiting. They were reclining in the tufted leather chairs with their feet up on a large, live-edge table made from a massive, century-old reclaimed Oak. As Blake entered, they sat up and grabbed three glasses filled with a neat dram from a bottle of 20-year-old bourbon. They handed one to Blake and motioned for him to sit in front of a freshly delivered basket of French fries. A warm smile spread across Blake's face.

"To Blake," Erin said, "for showing us that strength sometimes comes from the most unexpected places."

Raising their glasses for a toast, Leah spoke next. "We are proud of your journey, Blake. You have definitely earned a passing grade." Her voice was soft and reassuring, and Blake's eyes were misty with emotion.

Reaching behind the chair, Leah produced a framed certificate and handed it to Blake.

"We wanted you to have this," she said with a mischievous smile. Blake took the frame and studied it.

"Student of the Month." Blake laughed, cradling it to his chest. "I didn't think I could pass your finals, but I always knew I was the teacher's pet." The humor in his voice could not mask the grateful emotion spreading throughout the room.

"I hope you realize that this is more than a light-hearted accolade; it is a testament to the journey of transformation that had begun and will continue as you put your words into practice."

Leah raised her glass again, and they all participated in a moment of silent enjoyment.

After the glasses were empty and the dusk painted the office with hues of golden hour light, Blake found himself alone. The laughter, warmth, and aroma of the French fries still lingering, he held his glass, swirling the last cube of ice. His gaze fell once again upon the picture across the room. He walked over and picked it up to study it more closely, his fingers tracing the lines of the wooden frame.

"Dad," Blake murmured, his voice cutting through the silence and cracking with emotion. "I get it now. You were right. Leadership—true leadership—is about following well."

> "Leadership—true leadership—is about following well."

A single tear trickled down his cheek.

"You demonstrated this all my life, but I couldn't—or just wouldn't—see it. I hope you can forgive me for taking so long to learn."

He gently replaced the picture on his desk.

"I can only pray I have the wisdom and humility to follow well."

EPILOGUE
BLAKE'S FINAL NOTES TO ERIN

BLAKE'S JOURNAL NOTES TO ERIN

Duality of Roles: *Leadership and followership are two distinct but equal roles that contain both facets. This dichotomy highlights how easily one can move from leading to following, implying that both positions are critical to the leadership process.*

Active Participation: *In addition to carrying out tasks, a good follower actively engages in the leadership process by offering ideas and perspectives. This idea emphasizes how crucial followers are in forming leadership and influencing the path and accomplishments of the group or company.*

Learning and Development: *Mutual learning and development are essential components of true followership. As vital and dynamic as a leader's job, that of a follower emphasizes the reciprocal development and progress of both leaders and followers.*

Elevated Emotional Intelligence (EQ): *This trait, which includes self-awareness, intellectual humility, and the ability to rectify toxic leadership, is crucial for leaders as well as followers. This idea emphasizes how crucial EQ is to successfully juggling the two roles.*

Preventing Toxicity: *People can influence other leaders and stop the emergence of toxic qualities when they take on leadership roles by developing their EQ in followership. This emphasizes the proactive part that followers can play in preserving a positive workplace culture.*

Never Assume Knowledge: *The foundation of effective leadership is the idea that not everyone is as knowledgeable as you are. By promoting information exchange and a culture of ongoing education, this principle makes sure that everyone in the team is on the same page.*

Accept the Duality of Positions: *Encouraging people to alternate between leader and follower positions consciously helps them have a better awareness of the responsibilities and perspectives each role offers, improving team and organizational dynamics in general.*

Foster Continuous Learning: *Implementing initiatives such as "Leaders as Learners" shows that personal development and progress are anticipated and appreciated across the board, fostering a culture of adaptation and ongoing progress.*

The significance of transitioning from knowledge to understanding—which creates opportunities for empathy, creativity, and ultimately, transformation—is emphasized. This idea elevates comprehension depth over information acquisition alone.

Mission and Purpose Orbit: *To be an effective follower, one must operate in an orbit distinct from self-centeredness. This strategy emphasizes choices and activities grounded in the organization's overarching goals over individual agendas.*

REFERENCES

Bradberry, T., & Greaves, J. (2009). *Emotional Intelligence 2.0*. TalentSmart.

Gwinn, C., & Hellman, C. (2018). *Hope rising: How the science of hope can change your life*. Morgan James Publishing.

Kiel, F. (2015). *Return on character: The real reason leaders and their companies win*. Harvard Business Review Press.

ACKNOWLEDGMENTS

This is my seventh book, and the path to this page has differed from any of my other books. You could say it has been three years in the making. As I reflect on the journey, the list of people to acknowledge began manifesting into three buckets: collaborators, coaches, and counselors. What became quickly apparent is that these three groups of people are essential for doing life well.

Over the course of my last five books, my team of editors and designers, Mindi Bach and Stephanie Kemp, have been instrumental in the writing process. They have edited, designed, and believed in me, pushing me to reach my highest potential. This book, like the others, is a testament to the power of teamwork in bringing a story to life.

What makes this book slightly different from the others is the three years of study and research that preceded these pages, during which I was completing my doctorate in Organizational Intelligence and Leadership. The doctoral journey was impossible without a host of professors who have challenged me in magnificent ways to become a greater student of human behavior. Three professors stand out as vital coaches and, sometimes, counselors in my journey. Dr. Ryan Longnecker, Dr. Kristin Bledsoe, and my dissertation advisor, Dr. Jana Roberts. Each of these people has superpowers to change the world!

Other collaborators in life include the amazing team at The Encompass Group, led by my friend of twenty-five years, CEO and founder, John Luke Spitler, who is gifted in a host of ways to help others write their best stories. This talented and gifted group includes Monique Thompson, who keeps my life moving in the right direction, and Robert Rich, who has an amazing gift of pouring into people with great care.

According to Grammarly, the writing application, I have typed or reviewed over 20 million words since this journey began. That equates to a seemingly endless string of 4:30 am and late-night writing days that have consisted of an ocean of digital ink formatted in APA 7 style with 12pt Times New Roman.

As such, it is impossible to navigate that level of commitment without the support of family. In my case, I have been blessed beyond what I deserve. My bride of 34 years, Dee, has been my single biggest cheerleader and supporter, giving me the grace to allow for a plethora of missed date nights to finish research papers.

Additionally, my children have been beyond understanding. They cheer me along, celebrate each milestone along the way, and extend a measure of grace that is truly a gift from God.

TONY BRIDWELL

Tony Bridwell, Ed.D, MBA, is an organizational behaviorist with 25-plus years of experience working with global organizations related to employee experience and culture. As Chief Talent Officer for The Encompass Group, a leading people optimization company, he leads the Firm's organizational consulting practice. Most recently, Bridwell led the award-winning People Group function of the global tax and technology firm Ryan, LLC as their Chief People Officer. Before his role at Ryan, Bridwell was the Chief People Officer for Brinker International and a Senior Partner with the global culture consultancy Culture Partners.

Tony is an accomplished author of seven books, an international speaker, having presented in 44 countries, and a sought-after consultant and advisor specializing in purpose and culture. Dr. Bridwell was selected as the 2015 HR Executive of the Year by Dallas HR (the local SHRM affiliate), won the 2015 Strategic Leadership Award from Strategic Excellence HR, and was most recently recognized as a 2022 top 50 HR Professional by OnCon Icon Awards.

Having studied architecture, theology, and business, Tony has a Bachelor of Science in Business, a Master of Business Administration (MBA) degree, and a Doctorate in Organizational Intelligence. Tony is an adjunct professor at SMU in Dallas, teaching MBA students Executive Leadership. He is also dedicated to multiple organizations, including being a member of the Society for Human Resource Management (SHRM) and serving on the board of directors for Southwest Transplant Alliance. Tony is a living organ donor, and as such, his work with Southwest Transplant holds a special meaning as its purpose is to save lives through organ and tissue donation and transplantation.

Scan the QR code for more information on how to navigate your story personally, professionally, or organizationally.

More from Tony Bridwell

The Maker Series

The Difference Maker
The Kingmaker
The Newsmaker
The Changemaker

Saturday Morning Tea
The Do Over

amazon.com